John Eustace Prescott

Christian Hymns and Hymn Writers

A Course of Lectures. Second Edition

John Eustace Prescott

Christian Hymns and Hymn Writers
A Course of Lectures. Second Edition

ISBN/EAN: 9783337023010

Printed in Europe, USA, Canada, Australia, Japan

Cover: Foto ©Thomas Meinert / pixelio.de

More available books at **www.hansebooks.com**

CHRISTIAN HYMNS

AND

HYMN WRITERS.

Cambridge:
PRINTED BY C. J. CLAY, M.A. AND SON,
AT THE UNIVERSITY PRESS.

CHRISTIAN HYMNS

AND

HYMN WRITERS.

A COURSE OF LECTURES

BY

J. E. PRESCOTT, D.D.

ARCHDEACON AND CANON OF CARLISLE; EXAMINING CHAPLAIN
TO THE BISHOP OF CARLISLE; FORMERLY FELLOW OF
CORPUS CHRISTI COLLEGE, CAMBRIDGE.

SECOND EDITION, ENLARGED.

CAMBRIDGE:
DEIGHTON, BELL AND CO.
LONDON: GEORGE BELL AND SONS.
1886

TO

THE RIGHT REVEREND

HARVEY GOODWIN, D.D.
LORD BISHOP OF CARLISLE,

WITH WHOSE KIND ENCOURAGEMENT

THESE LECTURES WERE UNDERTAKEN

AND DELIVERED.

PREFACE TO THE SECOND EDITION.

In this edition, no important alteration has been made in the text of the Lectures. A few passages have been inserted which were previously omitted, and a few by way of explanation. Considerable additions have been made to the Notes, and the Appendix has been enlarged. It is hoped that this little work may thus become more useful as a book of reference. But the primary object was to present a fairly continuous narrative of a very extensive subject.

It is not generally recognised how many of our well-known hymns appear in their Latin forms in the ancient Service Books of the Church of England. Such Latin hymns and Sequences as have been referred to and occur in the Sarum or York Service Books have been specially marked in the Index.

In the three popular Hymnals to which the references have been given, there are above 160 hymns which are common to the three; and about 350 hymns which are to be found in at least two of them. Nearly all of these are among the hymns, in number about 800, mentioned in this book. I have again to thank many friends for kindly help and criticism.

J. E. P.

February, 1886.

PREFACE TO THE FIRST EDITION.

THESE *Lectures* lay no claim to form a set Treatise on Christian Hymns and Hymn Writers. They were delivered, in substance, in the ancient Fratry or Refectory of Carlisle Cathedral, and not without a view to the Cathedral Services. The object of the Lectures was to awaken a more thoughtful and intelligent interest in what is daily becoming a more important portion of public worship in England. It seemed to some who heard them that, if published, they might have this effect over a wider area.

I have here put into the shape of Lectures some of the results of searches prosecuted and notes made about Hymns during many years. The subject itself is indeed inexhaustible. But within so small a compass, no more than a mere outline could be given. I have endeavoured to compress as much reliable information as possible into the space at my disposal. The number of Christian hymns is to be calculated by thousands; and hymn writers have lived in so many and such different ages of the Christian era, that to establish a principle of selection affords no easy problem. Those hymns have, in the main, been chosen which are most frequently sung in Divine Service, and which are to be found in most of our Hymn Books. The brief account of the writers of these hymns has been given, as far as possible, in a consecutive and historical form. My desire has been to supply a continuous narrative rather than, what is more usual—a special essay or merely a book of reference.

Many excellent Church of England Hymnals are now in use; but references have only been given to the hymns in the three which have been ascertained to have the largest circulation, viz.—*Hymns Ancient and Modern*, *Church hymns* (S.P.C.K.) and *The Hymnal Companion*. These cover a wide field. There are few well-known hymns used in congregational singing which cannot be found in one of them. The variations made in hymns by compilers of Hymn Books are so numerous that exact reference is often a matter of difficulty. The lines quoted have, as a rule, been in the words of the author or translator named, and any serious difference has been noted.

The hymns given in the text have been generally selected as specimens of their respective authors, while additional hymns by the same author are often set out in the notes. In the Appendix will be found some hymns which it seemed impossible to pass by altogether, but which are, chiefly, by hymn-writers who have not been previously mentioned.

Except in a few instances, the subject matter of the hymns has not been discussed. Neither the time at my disposal nor the special object in view would admit of this. Moreover, the alterations made in hymns, even in the days of old, are so numerous and so arbitrary, that a boundless field of investigation and controversy at once opens before anyone who enters upon the discussion.

TABLE OF CONTENTS.

LECTURE I.

                                                                                               PAGE

ANCIENT HYMNS AND TRANSLATIONS 3

    Christian Unity.—The first Christian hymn.—Early Christian worship.—Jewish hymnody.—Pliny the younger.—The earliest Christian hymns.—Clement of Alexandria.—The Vesper hymn.—Ephrem the Syrian.—Arian hymn singing.—Synesius of Cyrene.—Ambrose of Milan.—Ambrosian hymns.—The Te Deum.—Hilary of Poitiers.—Prudentius.—Anatolius.—Venantius Fortunatus.—Gregory the Great.—Venerable Bede.—John Damascene.—Stephen the Sabaite.—Joseph of the Studium.—Theodulph of Orleans.—Sequences.—Robert II. of France.—The Veni Creator.—Bernard of Clairvaux.—Bernard of Clugny.—Bonaventura.—The Stabat Mater.—The Dies Iræ.—A mediæval lesson.

LECTURE II.

THE REFORMATION PERIOD 55

    Definition of the terms "psalm" and "hymn".—The "Period" a wide one.—Thomas Aquinas.—The Unreformed Service Books.—The Roman Hymnary.—Martin Luther.—Lutheran hymn singing.—Marot's Psalms.—The Old Version of the Psalms.—Bartholomäus Ringwaldt.—The King and Queen of Chorales.—The Thirty Years' War.—Gustavus Adolphus.—The Te Deum of Germany.—Lutheran hymn tunes.—The Electress Louisa.—Paul Gerhardt.—George Herbert.—"Jerusalem, my happy home."—John Milton.—Richard Baxter.—The New Version of the Psalms.—Joseph Addison.—Bishop Ken.

LECTURE III.

	PAGE
THE EIGHTEENTH CENTURY	109

Nonconformist hymnody.—Isaac Watts.—Alexander Pope.—Philip Doddridge.—The Paris Breviary hymns.—The Scotch Psalter.—Scotch Paraphrases.—The Moravian Brethren.—Count von Zinzendorf.—Moravian hymns.—John Wesley.—John Wesley's translations.—Methodist hymn singing.—Charles Wesley.—"Jesus Christ is risen to-day."—Thomas Olivers.—Augustus Toplady.—William Cowper.—The Olney hymns.—John Newton.

LECTURE IV.

MODERN HYMNOLOGY	165

Church of England hymnody.—Thomas Kelly.—James Montgomery.—The alteration of hymns.—Joseph Dacre Carlyle.—Henry Kirke White.—Richard Mant.—Reginald Heber.—Sir Robert Grant.—Henry Hart Milman.—John Keble.—The Christian Year.—Henry Francis Lyte.—Charlotte Elliott.—Frederick William Faber.—John Mason Neale.—Some well-known hymns and their authors.—John Henry Newman.—Frances Ridley Havergal.—Christian Unity.

APPENDIX.

ADDITIONAL HYMNS AND THEIR AUTHORS	221
INDEX OF ENGLISH HYMNS	263
,, ,, LATIN HYMNS AND SEQUENCES	281
,, ,, GERMAN HYMNS	285
GENERAL INDEX	287

CHRISTIAN HYMNS AND HYMN WRITERS.

LECTURE I.

ANCIENT HYMNS AND TRANSLATIONS.

LECTURE I.

HYMNS have always formed an important factor in Christian worship. As such, they must ever be a subject of interest. In this connection, and more especially in their bearing upon public worship, I propose to consider them. I shall not deal much in criticism, nor ventilate many of my own opinions. We shall, as we proceed, light upon many lands; we shall hear of the great principles of our faith as hymned in many tongues; we shall tread with rapid steps along many centuries of time; and we shall note the songs of many men, who were in race, in disposition, in manner of life, as opposite as the poles. But hence, I would prove a point. It is well to have before us a goal for our course of Lectures, a thesis to maintain. And I would prove the fundamental unity of Christian men. We may differ. It is, perhaps, as well that we should differ. We may part; but, as Christians, in Him we are one[1].

---

[1] "It is refreshing to turn aside from the divisions of the Christian world, and to rest for a little time in the sense of that inward unity, which, after all, subsists among all good Christians." Lord Selborne, *The Book of Praise.*—Preface.

The first Christian hymn of which we hear may be said to have been connected with the first act of Christian worship. It rose upon the night air in that upper room at Jerusalem, so sacred to us all. It was sung by our Blessed Lord and His eleven Apostles. The supper was over. "And when they had sung an hymn," S. Matthew tells us, "they went out into the Mount of Olives." We know what that "hymn" was. It was the last part of the Great Hallel, or Song of Praise. With this, the Passover Feast in general ended. It followed the third cup of the feast, "the cup of blessing." The "hymn" consisted of four psalms, cxv. to cxviii.

This brings before us the question, What is a hymn? We must for a time defer the answer. Definitions are somewhat straitlaced things. We must not tie ourselves up too tightly at present; but we must allow the word a far wider meaning than it now has in the hymn-books which we use.

Before advancing, it will be well for us to go back to those earliest Christian times, and trace very lightly some of the features of their public worship. The Christian Church was "heir to the grand inheritance of the Jewish Church." She was built upon the lines of the Temple and the synagogue. The worship of the Temple was chiefly local and sacrificial. But in the Jewish synagogue, it has been conclusively shewn, may be found the elements of Christian congregational worship[1].

At first, the little Christian community, even in Pagan cities, was a secession from the synagogue. The emissary of Christianity arrived, himself a Jew, perhaps an Apostle. The Jewish and Gentile converts formed themselves into a new society. They met for worship in some chamber, or some space open to the sky, or, as in times of persecution, some subterranean cemetery. But the model of worship, to which so many of them had been accustomed, they would naturally follow. As to what that model was, of what the synagogue service then consisted, much has of late become known. Its chief features were—Prayer and Benedictions, Reading of the Law and the Prophets, an Exposition, and Chanting. They chanted certain Psalms and other portions of the Scriptures, and, as well, certain sentences not found in the Scriptures, and often called the Hymnal Sentences[2]. Here, then, we have the germ of the future hymnody of the Church. The Christians

---

[1] See Freeman, *Principles of Divine Service*, vol. i. p. 62 *seq.* and Milman, *History of Christianity*, vol. ii. p. 17 *seq.*

[2] Here, I am indebted to the labours of Dr Ginsburg. The connection between Jewish and early Christian hymnody has not yet been sufficiently worked out. "Psalmody and hymnody were highly developed in the religious services of the Jews at this time," says Bishop Lightfoot, in his Commentary on the *Epistle to the Colossians;* see also his references there (Col. iii. 16).

would soon use hymns adapted to their faith in Christ. Such, doubtless, were the "hymns and spiritual songs[1]" spoken of by S. Paul (Ephes. v. 19; Col. iii. 16). Fragments of such hymns appear also to be quoted by S. Paul in his Epistles, in passages which are well known, and which have a distinct rhythm[2].

But we must pass on in our hymnal search away from Apostolic times. We emerge from the obscurity which hangs over the latter part of the first century of the Christian era. We soon find the traces we seek; and strangely enough the first are upon heathen soil. In the year of our Lord, 103, a Roman gentleman, known as Pliny the younger, was sent to be governor of the province of Pontus, in the north of Asia Minor. He was a nephew of Pliny, the famous naturalist, who was killed by that eruption of Vesuvius which destroyed the city of Pompeii. He was a man of great literary ability, and seems to have been fond of writing letters, and of preserving them. Ten books of his letters have come down to us. One letter has become famous. In it, Pliny writes to his master, the Emperor Trajan, for advice. In his new province, he had found a very

---

[1] On the distinction between these "hymns" and "spiritual songs," see Lecture ii. p. 56.
[2] See Ephes. v. 14; 1 Tim. iii. 16; vi. 15, 16; 2 Tim. ii. 11—13. In the Greek, the rhythmic character is very apparent.

troublesome set of people, called Christians. They were very numerous and very obstinate. The contagion of this superstition had spread to every age and rank and sex; and not in the large cities only, but also in the villages and open country. What was he to do with these Christians? He had punished some of them; but they were in such numbers. The difficulty was, he could find little or nothing against them. On strict examination, he learned, that they bound themselves not to do wrong; that it was their custom to meet on a fixed day before light, and to sing together in turn, or antiphonally, a hymn to Christ as God; then to separate, and after a time reassemble in order to eat together a simple and a harmless meal[1].

Here then we have a glimpse of early Christian worship; and we find, as it has been said, that "the first sound which reached the Pagan ear from the secluded sanctuaries of Christianity was a hymn to Christ as God[2]."

From this period, we might quote, had we the time, much evidence of Christian hymns being sung

---

[1] Pliny, Lib. x. *Epist.* 97.
[2] Milman, *Hist. of Christianity*. This custom is confirmed by the reference of Tertullian, writing at the end of the 2nd century (*Apologeticus*, c. 2), to this case—"he (Pliny) found in their religious services nothing but meetings at early morning for singing hymns to Christ as (or 'and') God."

during the next two centuries[1]. What then were these primitive hymns? Very early, no doubt, the hymns of the New Testament, such as the *Magnificat*, and *Benedictus* and *Nunc Dimittis*, were introduced. Soon, and as a Morning Hymn, we find the "Angelic Hymn," an earlier form of the *Gloria in Excelsis*, that is, the "Glory be to God on high" of our Communion Service; then, in varied forms, the *Gloria Patri* or Doxology; and then the *Trisagion, Ter Sanctus*[2] or "Holy, Holy, Holy, Lord God of Hosts[3]."

---

[1] Among the earliest instances, may be given the citation of the historian Eusebius from a still earlier writer (probably Hippolytus)—"Whatever psalms and odes were written by faithful brethren, from the beginning, hymn the Christ, the Word of God, speaking of Him as Divine."—*Hist. Eccles.* v. 28. Also Tertullian—dilating on the happiness of the Christian husband and wife—"Between the two echo psalms and hymns, and they mutually challenge one another which shall better sing to the Lord."—*Ad Uxor.* ii. 8; compare too *Apologeticus*, c. 39.

[2] Strickly speaking, the *Trisagion* was the hymn in the earlier portion of the Service in the Eastern Liturgies, the words being—"Holy God, Holy Mighty, Holy Immortal, have mercy upon us." But by some, this is taken to be only another form of the hymn in the latter portion of the Service called the "Triumphal" or "Seraphic Hymn" (compare Isaiah vi. 3), i.e. the *Ter Sanctus* of the Western Church.

[3] On the above points, see the numerous references given by Bingham, *Antiquities of the Christian Church*, Book xiv. chap. ii. and especially the passages in *The Apostolical Constitutions*, Book vii. chaps. 47, 48. There is a very ancient hymn in the famous manuscript, the *Codex Alexandrinus*, in the British Museum. It occurs at the end of the Psalms, and is headed "A Morning

But these, though they had a rhythm, had neither rhyme nor metre. And we hasten on to what, with some reason, has been termed "the earliest metrical Christian hymn." It is found in the writings of Clement of Alexandria, at the end of a Greek work called *The Tutor (Pædagogus)*, written between the years 190 and 195 A.D. It is a hymn for the young, entitled, "A Hymn of the Saviour Christ," addressed to Christ as King, and written in short anapæstic metre. Let us take a few lines from a translation:

> " King of saints, Almighty Word
> Of the Father, highest Lord :
> Wisdom's head and chief ;
> Assuagement of all grief ;
> Lord of all time and space ;
> Jesus, Saviour of our race.
> . . . . . .
> . . . . . .
> Let us, with hearts undefiled,
> Celebrate the mighty Child.

Hymn," Ύμνος ἑωθινός. The manuscript belongs, probably, to the 5th century; the hymn is very much older, although there is no authority for its ascription to Telesphorus, bishop of Rome, who died in 139 A.D. It begins with the words, "Glory to God in the highest," and is an early form of the *Gloria in Excelsis*. An account of it is given by Mr B. Harris Cowper in the Introduction to his edition of *Codex A. New Test.* p. xxvii. The original may be found in Daniel's *Thesaurus Hymnologicus*, ii. 289.

> We, Christ-born, the choir of peace,
> We, the people of His love,
> Let us sing, nor ever cease,
> To the God of peace above[1]."

Clement was a copious writer, and the head of the great Christian catechetical School at Alexandria, and the famous Origen was one of his pupils. Alexandria was, at the time, second to no city in the world in literary eminence; and inferior to Rome alone in magnificence. How changed now! A few years after this date, one of those terrible persecutions of the Christians broke out; and Clement fled from the world-renowned city, never to return. The last we hear of him is far away in Cappadocia, comforting a former pupil, Alexander, the future Bishop of Jerusalem, who was then a prisoner for the faith. Seventeen hundred years of Church controversy have rolled by since that day; and we look back with pleasure on that pure and simple hymn, on those noble words of faith in Christ, in "Jesus, Saviour of our race."

Another hymn whose author is unknown, quoted by the great writer, Basil[2], Bishop of Cæsarea in the 4th century, has tried to divide these early honours;

---

[1] By Dr W. L. Alexander. The original, which is largely a list of titles and epithets, is given in Daniel's *Thesaurus Hymnologicus*, vol. iii. p. 3.

[2] Basil, *De Spiritu Sancto*, c. 29.

but no doubt it is of a somewhat later date. It is still used in the evening office of the Eastern Church, and is called the Vesper or "Lamplighting" Hymn. The translation by John Keble begins—

"Hail, gladdening Light, of His pure glory poured,
Who is the immortal Father, heavenly, blest[1]."
(Ancient & Mod. 18)

Little more can be brought out of the darkness of the 3rd century. Probably, very few, if any, metrical hymns were in liturgical use. The music and singing were, we learn, of the simplest character, with very slight inflection of the voice. But with the 4th century, we enter upon what the Germans would call, the birth year-hundred, or birth century of liturgical Christian hymnody. We shall often note, as we go on, how productive of good hymns have been periods of religious excitement, and especially of religious controversy.

In the preceding century, the 3rd, there had been at Edessa, to the North-east of Syria, a Gnostic heretic, named Bardesanes. Gnosticism was a heresy which

---

[1] Φῶς ἱλαρὸν ἁγίας δόξης ἀθανάτου Πατρὸς. The above translation first appeared in *Lyra Apostolica*, under the signature γ. The original is in Daniel, *Thesaur. Hymnol.* iii. 5. The similar expressions in *The Apostolical Constitutions*, viii. 37, are worth comparing. There is a translation by E. W. Eddis in *Church Hymns* 25, beginning—
"O Brightness of the Eternal Father's face."
This hymn has been ascribed, but under a misapprehension, to Athenogenes, who was martyred about 175 A.D.

had in it much poetry; and Bardesanes was a great poet. He and his son, Harmonius, wrote a number of hymns, in Greek metres, and set them to popular secular melodies. With these, they completely bewitched the ears of the Syrian Christians, and increased the influence of this sect. For many years these heretical hymns retained their great popularity. So attractive were they, that, we learn, the very girls and children knew them by heart, and sang them at their work and at their play. But in the 4th century, there came to Edessa a Christian of distinguished ability, and a keen controversialist, named Ephrem the Syrian. He determined to fight these heretics with their own weapons; and he proved more than a match for them. He composed a large number of orthodox hymns for public and private use, and set them to the same popular tunes. He also trained choirs of young women who sang these hymns in chorus. So beautiful were his poems, and so successful were his efforts, that it is said the whole city flocked to listen; and the heretical strains of Bardesanes were for ever driven out of the field. Moreover, from that period, metrical hymns found their place in the services of the Syrian Churches of the East.

Ephrem was a most voluminous writer, and much has come down to us in Greek and Syriac, including many hymns. Some of these hymns have been literally translated from the Syriac¹; but I am not aware that any of the translations occupy a place in our hymnbooks. The *Testament* of Ephrem, his last work, is also written in the form of a hymn, and contains some curious passages. He tells us that, when he was quite a child on his mother's knee, he saw in a dream what became a reality:—"From my tongue there grew a vine which bore clusters of grapes without end, and leaves without number. Those clusters were sermons, those leaves were hymns, and God was the giver. To Him be glory for His grace." I have said that Ephrem was great in controversy. He writes thus—"Throughout my whole life, neither by night nor day have I reviled any one, nor striven with any one. But in their assemblies, I have disputed with those who deny the faith. For if a wolf is entering the fold, and the dog goes not

---

[1] Translations may be found in *Select Metrical Hymns and Homilies of Ephræm Syrus* by Rev. H. Burgess, 1853. These metrical hymns were written chiefly in lines of seven syllables, and, although they do not rhyme or scan, were thus easily set to music. In Mrs Charles' *Voice of Christian Life in Song* there are a few renderings of the German version of those given by Daniel (*Thesaur. Hymnol.* iii. 45). Mrs Elizabeth Charles (who wrote *The Chronicles of the Schonberg-Cotta Family*) is also the author of the hymns—

"Is thy cruse of comfort wasting? rise and share it with another."
(*Hymnal Comp.* 374)

and—

"Toss'd with rough winds, and faint with fear."
(*Hymnal Comp.* 468)

out and barks, the master beats the dog. But a wise man hates no one; or if he hate at all, he hates only a fool." We might learn some lessons from the first Christian hymnologist, Ephrem the Syrian.

The next, and somewhat similar, scene takes us to Constantinople, then the capital of the world, the new Rome of the East. At the Council of Nicæa in A. D. 325, the famous heretic, Arius, who had denied the Divinity of our Lord, was condemned, and the main part of our Nicene Creed was put forth. Arius had been rebuked by his great opponent, Athanasius, for the light character of certain hymns which he had set to popular tunes, as well as for the doctrines they contained. The Arians might be condemned, but they flourished greatly. And when, more than seventy years after, the renowned John Chrysostom arrived as Bishop of Constantinople, he found a strange state of things. The Arians had, some years before, been forbidden by the Emperor Theodosius to have places of worship within the city[1]. But, on Saturdays, and Sundays, and great festivals, they were in the habit of assembling outside the gates, then coming into the city in procession at sunset; and all night, in the porticoes and open places, singing Arian hymns and anthems with choruses. Chrysostom feared that many of the

---

[1] Compare Gibbon, *Decline and Fall of the Roman Empire*, chap. xxvii.

simple and ignorant people would be drawn from the faith. He therefore organised, at the cost of the Empress Eudoxia, wife of Arcadius, nightly processions of orthodox hymn singers, who carried crosses and lights, and with music and much pomp rivalled the efforts of the heretics. Riots and bloodshed were the consequence. The chief officer of the Empress was wounded; and very soon an imperial edict put a stop to Arian hymn-singing in public. The use, however, of hymns in the nocturnal services of the Church became established; and this at once led up to a much freer and more constant use of them in Divine Service generally. We can scarcely fail to note here, especially in these days, what a strange habit history has of repeating herself from time to time.

During this century, many hymns were written for the Eastern Church, by Methodius, Bishop of Tyre, and Bishop Gregory Nazianzen, the predecessor of Chrysostom, and by others; of these hymns, few came into more modern use. But before we turn to the far West of that day, I would touch upon one hymn. Many have heard of Synesius of Cyrene, Bishop of Ptolemais in North Africa. At all events, he is known to the readers of Kingsley's *Hypatia*, where a life-like sketch is given of him—the Squire Bishop who talked philosophy and religion at night, and hunted his hounds with equal zest in the morning. We should scarcely suspect him of being the author of, among others, that most spiritual hymn—

"Lord Jesus, think on me."
(*Ancient & Mod.* 185)

The translation is by Rev. A. W. Chatfield[1]—

"Lord Jesus, think on me,
And purge away my sin;
From earthborn passions set me free,
And make me pure within.

. . . .

Lord Jesus, think on me,
Nor let me go astray;
Through darkness and perplexity
Point Thou the heavenly way.

Lord Jesus, think on me,
That, when the flood is passed,
I may the eternal brightness see,
And share Thy joy at last."

There are those who knew the somewhat secular manner of Charles Kingsley at times in public, and also the deep piety of his more spiritual moments, and they have not failed to trace some likeness in character to the Squire Bishop, Synesius of Cyrene[2].

---

[1] In nine stanzas, from *Songs and Hymns of Earliest Greek Christian Poets*, 1875.

[2] Synesius was made Bishop of Ptolemais A.D. 410. Among his extant writings, there are ten hymns.

It is remarkable, that the action of the Arians of the West led up, about the same time, or a little before, to the same result as that produced by the Arians of the East, viz. the establishment of metrical hymns as a constant part of Divine Service. We go, not to Rome, but to her rival in Italy at the time, to Milan, the capital of North Italy, the Athens of the West. We meet two of the greatest names in Ecclesiastical history, Augustine and Ambrose. The Church at Milan was rent by strife between the Orthodox and the Arian sympathizers. A violent contest arose on a vacancy in the bishopric. Ambrose was the consular magistrate of the province at the time, an able, high-minded Christian man. He had come down to the church to keep the peace between the contending parties, when a cry arose amid the tumult, said to have been uttered by a child, "Ambrose for bishop." The cry caught the popular ear. The ardour of the people at length prevailed; and he became perhaps the greatest bishop that the world has seen (A. D. 375). After no slight experience of his strength, the Emperor Theodosius said, "I have known no bishop, except Ambrose." He is one of the few ecclesiastics of whom the historian Gibbon speaks with respect.

The Arians, however, continued their efforts, and they were strongly supported by the court. Ten years after Ambrose had come to the see, a demand was made by the Empress-mother Justina, that one of the basilicas or churches of Milan should be given up for Arian worship. Ambrose promptly refused. A period of terrible excitement followed. The imperial troops were sent to enforce obedience. Ambrose and the people occupied the basilica day after day. So great was his influence, that, when at length the soldiers crowded in, they cried out—they had come to pray and not to fight. The court party was worsted.

The next year, the angry Empress determined to remove Ambrose. But the devoted people took the alarm. In immense numbers, they gathered about him, and kept guard day and night in the Church, ready if need be, to die with their Bishop. Ambrose preached to them, and gave them psalms and hymns and, in some cases, tunes of his own to sing, in order to cheer and sustain them. The court gave way. Again Ambrose was victorious.

Among those anxious worshippers, was Monica, the mother of the great Augustine. Augustine himself tells us—"at this time it was instituted that, after the manner of the Eastern Churches, hymns and psalms should be sung, lest the people should grow weary and faint through their sorrow; which custom has ever since been retained, and is imitated by almost all the congregations throughout the world[1]." We learn too, from Paulinus,

---

[1] Augustine, *Confessions*, Book ix. chap. 7.

the secretary of Ambrose, and from others, that to these services, thus organised, we owe the introduction of hymns and antiphons into the regular Offices of the Western Churches.

Augustine describes how deeply he himself was moved by the singing of these "hymns and canticles" about a year afterwards in the Church at Milan. We are anxious to know what they were. Nearly one hundred extant hymns are called "Ambrosian." Most of them belong to that period, or to the next century, and are in imitation of him. About twelve metrical hymns are with good authority ascribed to Ambrose. Augustine distinctly quotes four as being by Ambrose. To one, an Evening hymn, he refers under very touching circumstances. It was the night after the funeral of his mother Monica, to whom he was so deeply attached. He had been overwhelmed with grief. "As I lay alone upon my bed," he says, "there came into my mind those true verses of Thy Ambrose, for Thou art—

> Maker of all things! God most High!
> Great Ruler of the starry sky!
> Robing the day in beauteous light;
> In sweet repose the quiet night,
> That sleep may our tired limbs restore,
> And fit for toil and use once more;
> May gently soothe the careworn breast,
> And lull our anxious griefs to rest[1]."

---

[1] Augustine, *Confessions*, Book ix. chap. 12.

That Latin hymn—

        Deus, Creator omnium,

has been sung many a time in this Cathedral in days gone by[1]; and very many of these ancient hymns are to be found in the old Service Books of the Church of England.

We must only refer to one or two others, of which we find translations in our hymn books. The Morning hymn—

        Splendor Paternæ gloriæ,
        "O Jesu, Lord of heavenly grace."
        (Ancient & Mod. 2; *Church Hymns* 10; *Hymnal Comp.* 2)

translated by John Chandler[2].

The Evening hymn—

        O Lux beata, Trinitas,
        "O Trinity, most blessed Light."
        (Ancient & Mod. 14)

The fine Ascensiontide hymn—

        Æterne Rex, Altissime,
        "O Lord most High, Eternal King."
        (Ancient & Mod. **144**)

And, most probably, the Morning Hymn—

        Jam lucis orto sidere,
        "Now that the daylight fills the sky."
        (Ancient & Mod. **1**; *Church Hymns* 9)

all translated by J. M. Neale.

---

[1] In the *Sarum Breviary*, it was appointed to be used at Vespers on Saturdays, during a part of the year.

[2] See Appendix, page 236.

This last hymn is said to have been sung by the deathbed of William the Conqueror in 1087; but the following would be the more correct account. As the king lay on his deathbed at Rouen, on a Thursday morning in September, he asked why the bell of the Cathedral sounded. He was told that it rang for Prime. William lifted up his eyes to heaven, and prayed; and soon after his soul passed away[1]. The hymn sung that day at the Hour of Prime would be—

Jam lucis orto sidere.

There is another, a grand Advent hymn, of Ambrose, quoted by Augustine[2] as having been sung in the Church at that date—

Veni Redemptor gentium[3],
"O come, Redeemer of mankind, appear."
(Ancient & Mod. 55)

a free translation by D. T. Morgan.

---

[1] Compare Freeman, *Norman Conquest*, iv. 712.

[2] *Sermon.* 372. The two other hymns, quoted by Augustine and not mentioned in the text, are—"Æterne rerum Conditor" *Retractat.* i. 21, and "Jam surgit hora tertia," *De Naturâ*, cap. 63.

[3] This also is in the *Sarum Breviary*. A fine translation by Johann Franck (died 1677) begins—

Komm, Heidenheiland, Lösegeld,

of which the original is in Bunsen's *Gesang- und Gebet-Buch*, No. 19, and an English translation—

"Redeemer of the nations, come."

by Miss Winkworth in *Lyra Germanica*, 1st series, p. 188.

Of hymns *ascribed* to Ambrose, or Ambrosian, there are besides translations of several in our hymn books[1].

---

[1] Such as these are well known—

Ad coenam Agni providi,
"The Lamb's high banquet let us share."
(*Ancient & Mod.* 128)

Æterna Christi munera,
"The eternal gifts of Christ the King."
(*Ancient & Mod.* 430; *Church Hymns* 193)

Aurora lucis rutilat,
"Light's glittering morn bedecks the sky."
(*Ancient & Mod.* 126)

Deus, Tuorum militum,
"O God, Thy soldiers' great reward."
(*Ancient & Mod.* 442)

Te lucis ante terminum,
"Before the ending of the day."
(*Ancient & Mod.* 15; *Church Hymns* 9)

translated mainly by J. M. Neale.

Christe, Redemptor omnium,
"O Christ, Redeemer of our race."
(*Ancient & Mod.* 57)

translated by Sir Henry Baker.

Christe, qui Lux es et Dies,
"O Christ, Who art the Light and Day."
(*Ancient & Mod.* 95)

translated by W. J. Copeland.

and—

Vox clara ecce intonat,
"Hark, a thrilling voice is sounding."
(*Ancient & Mod.* 47; *Church Hymns* 67)

translated by Edward Caswall, or rather from the *Roman Breviary* version of this hymn—

En clara vox redarguit.

The Te Deum.

All these hymns were written in metre, but not in rhyme, like the later Latin hymns. We learn from Ambrose himself[1], that the singing of the psalms, and probably of these hymns, was antiphonal or responsive. All were congregational; the harmony, he says, rolling along like the noise of the waves of the sea.

One word on that grandest unmetrical hymn, the Te Deum. We know that Ambrose has, on no good grounds, been said to be its author. The earliest notice of it yet discovered is some 150 years afterwards, in the Rule of Cæsarius, Bishop of Arles, about A.D. 527. There the Te Deum is mentioned as one among other psalms and hymns, well known and of long standing; but portions of it, undoubtedly, belong to a much earlier date than this; and some may be traced to the writings of the Eastern Church even in the 3rd or 4th century[2].

---

[1] Ambrose, *Hexaemeron*, iii. 5.

[2] For instance, in the "Triumphal Hymn" (see page 8) of the so-called Liturgy of S. James, there are the very words of the clauses— "Holy, Holy, Holy, Lord God Almighty : Heaven and earth are full of Thy glory." Also, in the "Morning Hymn" of the *Codex Alexandrinus* (see page 9), there are words almost identical with the clauses—"Day by day &c."; "Vouchsafe, O Lord &c.": "Lord, let thy mercy &c." The antiquity of another portion is shewn by the following passage of Cyprian (*De Mortalitate*) A.D. 250—"There is the glorious company of the Apostles; there is the number of the prophets exulting; there is the innumerable multitude of martyrs." In the *Sarum Breviary*, the Te Deum is to be said, as a rule, on the Lord's Day, at Matins, after the Lesson of the Gospel.

Like the most ancient compositions of the early Church, it appears to be a hymn to the Holy Trinity, while the great central thought is the redemptive work of Christ. In its noble words, the feelings of men have ever found utterance, alike in times of deep sorrow or of supreme exultation.

Some years before the time of Ambrose, hymns appear to have been written in the Western Church; and Hilary, Bishop of Poitiers in France, A. D. 354, is spoken of as "the first Latin hymn writer[1]." His Morning hymn—

> Lucis Largitor splendide,
> "Thou bounteous Giver of the light."

is, perhaps, the best known. It was sent, together with an Evening hymn, in a letter to his daughter Abra, by Hilary when he was in exile. "It is singular," says Dr Cazenove, "that the earliest Latin hymn to which we are able to assign a name as that of its author, should be the work of that Father of the Church who gave us the earliest treatise upon the doctrine of the Trinity and the first commentary upon a Gospel[2].

Our materials now become so abundant, that hence-

---

[1] By Isidore of Seville, about A.D. 630.
[2] *S. Hilary of Poitiers and S. Martin of Tours*, 1883, by J. G. Cazenove, D.D.

forth we must, in the main, confine ourselves to those hymns and their authors which are most familiar to us. Content with having traced the rise of Christian hymnody in the East and West, and marked its entry into Divine Service, we must not tarry to follow its course in the daily and other Offices of the Church, a subject itself of no small interest.

At the very beginning of the next, the 5th century, but towards the end of his life, a number of very sweet hymns were written by Prudentius. He was a native of Spain, born A.D. 348, a lawyer and a judge; and later, he held a high military appointment at the Court, given to him by the Emperor. When he was more advanced in years, at the age of fifty-seven, he spoke of the emptiness of the world's honours and of his determination to devote the remainder of his life to God. It was at this period that he wrote his hymns. The great critic Bentley styled him "the Horace and Virgil of the Christians." Two of his hymns are well known by translations. The Christmas hymn—

> Corde natus, ex Parentis,
> Ante mundi exordium.

> "Of the Father's love begotten,
> Ere the worlds began to be."

(*Ancient & Mod.* **56**; *Church Hymns* **84**; *Hymnal Comp.* **74**)

translated by J. M. Neale and Sir Henry Baker.

And the Epiphany hymn—

> O sola magnarum urbium,
> "Earth has many a noble city;
> Bethlehem, thou dost all excel."
> *(Ancient & Mod. 76)*

translated by Edward Caswall[1].

There is a beautiful Greek hymn, written about the middle of that 5th century, and known to all. Its author is Anatolius—

> "The day is past and over;
> All thanks, O Lord, to Thee."
> *(Ancient & Mod. 21; Church Hymns 31; Hymnal Comp. 22)*

The translator, Dr Neale, says that it is a great favourite in the Greek Isles at the present day.—"It is to the scattered hamlets of Chios and Mitylene what Bishop Ken's Evening Hymn is to the villages of our own land." Anatolius was Bishop of Constantinople, and joint president of the great Church Council of Chalcedon (A. D. 451) when the see of Constantinople was made equal in dignity to that of Rome. He also wrote the spirited hymn—

---

[1] To Aurelius Clemens Prudentius, to give his name in full, is also due the hymn for Innocents' Day—

> Salvete flores martyrum,
> "Sweet flowerets of the martyr band."
> *(Ancient & Mod. 68)*

translated by Sir H. Baker. These are all taken from the *Liber Cathemerinōn* of Prudentius.

"Fierce was the wild billow;
Dark was the night."
(Hymnal Comp. 534)

This is the third stanza of Neale's translation—

"Jesu, Deliverer!
Come Thou to me:
Soothe Thou my voyaging
Over Life's sea.
Thou, when the storm of Death
Roars, sweeping by,
Whisper, O Truth of Truth
—'Peace! It is I.'"

There are two very famous Latin hymns written by Venantius Fortunatus, who died in A. D. 609, Bishop of Poitiers in France. An Italian by birth, he was in early life one of those wandering minstrels of the period, who passed from place to place earning a livelihood by their skill in verse. In Southern Gaul, he became a great favourite, and was persuaded by Rhadegunda, Queen of the Franks, who presided over a monastic institution at Poitiers, to join her there and to be ordained. "This world-famous hymn," as Dr Neale calls it—

Vexilla Regis prodeunt,
"The Royal banners forward go,
The Cross shines forth in mystic glow."
(Ancient & Mod. 96; Church Hymns 118)

was a processional hymn, but afterwards used on Passion Sunday, the 5th Sunday in Lent. It was composed on the occasion of the reception of certain relics by Gregory, Bishop of Tours, and Queen Rhadegunda, previous to the consecration of a church at Poitiers. The other hymn is—

> Pange lingua gloriosi proelium certaminis,
> "Sing, my tongue, the glorious battle;
> Sing the last, the dread affray."
> *(Ancient & Mod.* 97; *Church Hymns* 117)

to be carefully distinguished from one by Thomas Aquinas with a similar Latin beginning[1].

In the sixth century, the most prominent ecclesiastical figure was that of Gregory the Great, Pope and Bishop of Rome. He devoted much personal care to the music of the Church. He is said to have himself

---

[1] See page 58. The above translations are founded on those of J. M. Neale; those in *Church Hymns* begin respectively—

> "The Royal banner is unfurled."

and—

> "Sing, my tongue, the Saviour's glory."

The hymn for the Annunciation, by the same translator—

> Quem terra, pontus, aethera,
> "The God, Whom earth and sea and sky,"
> *(Ancient & Mod.* 449)

and the Easter hymn—Salve festa dies (see Appendix, page 261) are also ascribed to Venantius Fortunatus. This last hymn is said by Daniel (iv. 143) to have been sung by Jerome of Prague when at the stake in 1416.

instructed the singers, and to have introduced a new style of chanting, distinct from that of Ambrose, and which still bears his name. When Gregory sent the famous Christian mission under Augustine, in A. D. 597, to the shores of Southern Britain, he did not forget the help that music would afford. Augustine was accompanied by a band or school of choristers; and their solemn chanting was not without its effect on the Saxon King, Ethelbert, and Bertha, his Christian Queen. Nine hymns are with fairly good authority ascribed to Gregory. Perhaps, the best known is the Lent hymn—

> Audi benigne Conditor,
> "O merciful Creator, hear;
> To us in pity bow Thine ear."
> *(Ancient & Mod.* 87; *Church Hymns* 109)

translated by J. M. Neale[1].

---

[1] Another hymn of Gregory—
> Primo dierum omnium,
> "On this day when days began."
> *(Church Hymns* 37)

is translated by Rev. J. Ellerton. The somewhat similar hymn—
> "On this day, the first of days."
> *(Ancient & Mod.* 34)

is translated by Sir H. Baker from one in the *Le Mans Breviary*—
> Die parente temporum.

The Lent hymn—
> Ecce tempus idoneum,
> "Lo! now is our accepted day."
> *(Ancient & Mod.* 88)

translated by J. M. Neale, is ascribed to Gregory; also the

We turn again for a time with pleasure to the shores of what we now call "Old England." Away on the east coast, probably at Jarrow on the Tyne, where he studied and died, was born in A.D. 673 the Venerable Beda or Bede. His great literary attainments and the long list of works which he produced would be very remarkable in any age. But, strange as it may sound, probably nowhere in the world would he have had greater opportunities for study at that time than in the sister monasteries of Wearmouth and Jarrow to which he belonged. Among his many writings is one entitled, *A Book of Hymns, in several sorts of Metre, or Rhyme.* These are in Latin; but he also wrote some Anglo-Saxon hymns. Bede speaks with delight of his care for "the daily singing in the Church;" and he died in the act of chanting, on the evening before Ascension Day A.D. 735, with the words of the *Gloria Patri* upon his lips. Perhaps the two best known of his hymns are—

>Precursor altus luminis,
>"The great forerunner of the morn,
>The herald of the Word, is born."
>*(Ancient & Mod. 415)*

Evening hymn—
>Lucis Creator optime,
>"Blest Creator of the light."
>*(Ancient & Mod. 38)*

translated by J. Chandler (and much altered), but the latter belongs, at the latest, to the 5th century.

for S. John Baptist's Day, translated by J. M. Neale; and—

> Hymnum canentes martyrum,
> "A hymn for martyrs sweetly sing."

for Innocents' Day[1].

For our next hymn poet, we pass by a long step from the green shores of England to the desolate region on the west of the Dead Sea. Here, to the monastery of S. Sabas, now called Mar Saba, there retired from the world John Damascene, so named from his native place, Damascus. And here he died about A.D. 780, "the last" as he is termed by Gibbon, "of the Greek Fathers." He played an important part in the literary warfare of the age, and boldly entered the lists against Leo, the Emperor of the East[2]. Just as the parched

---

[1] Another, a hymn for the Ascension, is—
> Hymnum canamus gloriæ,
> "Sing we triumphant songs of praise."

An excellent and concise account of Bede and his writings, written by Rev. G. F. Browne, of Cambridge, is to be found in *The Fathers for English Readers* (S. P. C. K.).

[2] John Mansur, as he was otherwise called, attacked with great vigour, in his *Orations*, the Byzantine Emperor Leo, when the latter issued his decrees against the iconoclasts. He wrote with energy also against the Muhammadans of his day, among whom he lived. These, with others of his writings, are extant. To him is due the famous saying:—"The well being of the State pertains to princes, but the ordering of the Church to pastors and teachers." Compare Robertson, *History of the Christian Church*, Book iv. chap. 4. Milman, *Latin Christianity*, Book iv. chap. 7.

traveller in some sandy desert dreams of green fields and purling streams, so, we can fancy, John of Damascus, lately the fierce warrior in the great Iconoclastic controversy, now the aged and weary anchorite in this barren and dry land, bursting forth into the popular hymn of to-day—

> "Those eternal bowers
> Man hath never trod,
> Those unfading flowers
> Round the throne of God:
> Who may hope to gain them
> After weary fight?
> Who at length attain them
> Clad in robes of white?
>
> . . . . . .
> . . . . . .
>
> While we do our duty,
> Struggling through the tide,
> Whisper Thou of beauty
> On the other side.
> What though sad the story
> Of this life's distress:
> Oh, the future glory!
> Oh, the loveliness."
>
> (*Church Hymns* 524 : *Hymnal Comp.* 234)

This was written 'For All Saints,' and is translated by J. M. Neale, in his *Hymns of the Eastern Church*.

Dean Stanley gives a vivid description of Easter Day

morning at Athens, the joyous congratulations, the exulting shouts "Christ is risen," "Christ is risen," and the chanting of what he calls "the glorious old hymn of victory." That "old hymn of victory" is by this same John Damascene:—

"The Day of Resurrection,
Earth, tell it out abroad."
(Ancient and Mod. 132; Church Hymns 137; Hymnal Comp. 186)

It is part of his Canon for Easter Day, called "The Golden Canon."

He also wrote the hymn for Low Sunday, or Eastertide, beginning—

"Come, ye faithful, raise the strain
Of triumphant gladness."
(Ancient & Mod. 133; Church Hymns 135)

The translations are both by J. M. Neale.

Another hymn, now also deservedly popular, was written by his nephew, Stephen the Sabaite, an inmate of the same monastery of S. Sabas—

"Art thou weary, art thou languid?
Art thou sore distressed?"
(Ancient & Mod. 254; Church Hymns 333; Hymnal Comp. 142)

translated by J. M. Neale.

One more of these Greek hymn poets should be mentioned here, S. Joseph of the Studium, who lived in the early part of the 9th century. He was a Sicilian who, after many adventures, retired to the great abbey of the Studium at Constantinople; he was the most prolific of Greek hymn writers. To him and to Dr Neale, we owe "The Pilgrims of Jesus"—

> "O happy band of pilgrims,
> If onward ye will tread."
> *(Ancient & Mod.* 224; *Church Hymns* 468; *Hymnal Comp.* 325)

and "The Return Home"—

> "Safe home, safe home in port,
> Rent cordage, shattered deck."
> *(Church Hymns* 492; *Hymnal Comp.* 486)

which was sung to Dr Neale when he lay upon his death-bed[1].

An interesting legend is given concerning a hymn written at the beginning of the 9th century—the hymn for Palm Sunday—

Gloria, laus et honor Tibi sit Rex, Christe, Redemptor,
> "All glory, laud, and honor,
> To Thee, Redeemer, King,"
> *(Ancient & Mod.* 98; *Church Hymns* 113; *Hymnal Comp.* 160)

translated by J. M. Neale. Theodulph had been made

---

[1] To these should be added—
"Let our choir new anthems raise."
(Ancient & Mod. 441; *Church Hymns* 200)
and—
"Stars of the morning, so gloriously bright."
(Ancient & Mod. 423; *Church Hymns* 186; *Hymnal Comp.* 364)

Bishop of Orleans by the Emperor Charlemagne. His son, the Emperor Lewis, suspecting Theodulph of conspiring against the throne, deprived him of his see, and cast him into prison in Metz. On Palm Sunday, the Emperor, his court, and the clergy went in solemn procession through the city of Metz to the church. As they passed the window of his prison, Theodulph, or choristers instructed by him, sang this hymn which he had composed. The Emperor was so struck by the hymn and by the devotion of the moment, that he ordered the immediate release of the Bishop. Ever since, it has been sung on Palm Sunday in the Western Church[1].

Before touching upon a few of the most celebrated hymns of this period, I will just mention that the so-called "Alleluiatic Sequence"—

> Cantemus cuncti melodum nunc, Alleluia,
> "The strain upraise of joy and praise, Alleluia."
> *(Ancient & Mod. 295; Church Hymns 516; Hymnal Comp. 528)*

translated by J. M. Neale, was written by Godescalcus, or Gottshalk, of the monastery of S. Gall, near Constance,

---

[1] See Daniel, *Thesaurus Hymnol.* i. 216. The hymn is written in alternate hexameters and pentameters. It is given in *The Sarum Processional*, to be sung outside on the south of the Church when going in procession, the first verse to be repeated as a chorus.

who died about A.D. 950, and of whom little more is known[1].

But what is a Sequence? In the Service of the Western Church, the *Alleluia*, the "Praise ye the Lord," followed the *Gradual*, or Anthem sung between the Epistle and the Gospel. It had become the custom to prolong the last syllable of the *Alleluia* to a great number of notes, while the reader of the Gospel went to his place. A monk of this same monastery of S. Gall, named Notker Balbulus, who died about A.D. 912, conceived the idea of replacing this interminable syllable of the *Alleluia* by words set to the series of notes[2]. This from its position and form, being in rhythmical prose, was called a "Sequence" or "Prose". These Sequences thus came into common use. One written by Notker is familiar to us—*Media vita in morte sumus*. From it were taken the words in our solemn Burial Service—"In the midst of life we are in death"—with the sentences following. It is said to have been suggested to Notker as he watched the

---

[1] Early in the 9th century, there was a German monk of the same name, who took up such strong predestinarian views that he was condemned as a heretic; with him our writer must not be confounded (see Milman, *Latin Christianity*, Book viii. Chap. 5). Translations of two more of his Sequences are given in Neale's *Mediæval Hymns*, p. 34.

[2] As a rule, the *Alleluia* was not sung between Septuagesima and Easter; see page 61.

Robert II. of France.

samphire gatherers on the cliffs of S. Gall pursue their dangerous calling[1].

A king, and a very weak king, Robert II. of France, was the author of what Archbishop Trench styles "the loveliest of all the hymns in the whole circle of Latin sacred poetry." It is called also "The Golden Sequence," and is in metrical form:—

> Veni, Sancte Spiritus,
> "Come, Thou Holy Spirit, come;
> And from Thy celestial home."
> *(Ancient & Mod. 156)*

translated by Edward Caswall[2].

It is said that at the famous dispute between Luther and Dr Eck in the Castle of Leipsic, before the Elector of Saxony, Duke George, on June 27th, 1519, pro-

---

[1] According to others, as he saw the workmen throwing a bridge across a dangerous torrent near the monastery. This Sequence was for a time used as a battle song; Luther made a metrical version of it which was much used as a funeral hymn—

> Mittin wir im Leben sind
> Mit dem Tod umfangen.

In the *Sarum Breviary* it is given to be sung as an Antiphon at Compline on the 3rd Sunday in Lent.

[2] The translation by J. M. Neale—

> "Come, Thou Holy Paraclete,"
> *(Hymnal Comp. 251)*

is inferior to this. By some, the hymn is supposed to have been written by Cardinal Stephen Langton, Archbishop of Canterbury, A.D. 1207.

ceedings began with a Latin oration. After this discourse, music resounded through the hall, and, whilst the whole assemblage knelt, the ancient hymn "Veni, Sancte Spiritus" was solemnly chanted[1].

Robert II. wrote many hymns and chants, and was an excellent musician, but quite unequal to deal with those turbulent times, or that turbulent woman, his wife, Constantia. This hymn seems to tell of the sorrows and troubles through which he had passed. He was in the habit of going to the Church of S. Denis, where he was afterwards buried in the year 1031; there crowned and in his royal robes, he used to direct the choir, and sing in the Service with the monks.

It may be well to notice, in this connection, the celebrated hymn—

Veni, Creator Spiritus.

It is known to us best by the rendering in the Prayer Book—

"Come, Holy Ghost, our souls inspire,
And lighten with celestial fire."

(*Ancient & Mod.* 157; *Church Hymns* 346; *Hymnal Comp.* 537)

The authorship has been ascribed to the Emperor Charlemagne, to Gregory the Great and to others, but on no good authority. The earliest recorded instance of its use was in A. D. 898, at the translation of some

---

[1] Hagenbach, *History of the Reformation.*

The Veni Creator.

relics, as mentioned in the *Annals* of the Benedictines[1]; it was probably written during that century. It has been long used throughout Western Christendom on occasions of special solemnity—the coronation of kings, the consecration of bishops, the ordination of priests, the celebration of synods and the election of popes. It is the only metrical hymn, out of the many in use before the Reformation in the Church of England, which has been retained in our Book of Common Prayer. The translation noted above appeared in the Ordinal of the Prayer Book in 1662. It was, there is little doubt, the work of Bishop Cosin, who was made Bishop of Durham in 1660, and is found in his *Collection of Private Devotions* (1627).

The second and longer rendering in our Book of Common Prayer appeared in the earlier Prayer Book of 1552, when the Ordinal was first added—

"Come, Holy Ghost, eternal God,
Proceeding from above."

---

[1] See Daniel, *Thesaurus Hymnol.* i. 214; iv. 124. In the *Sarum Breviary*, it is directed to be used at the Hour of Terce for the first three days during the Octave of Pentecost; it is also to be sung by the priest at the commencement of the "Ordinary of the Mass." The original has thirty-two stanzas; the last is—

Sit laus Patri cum Filio
Sancto simul Paraclito:
Nobisque mittat Filius
Charisma Sancti Spiritus.

But Bishop Cosin has introduced in his last four lines part of the version of the *Pontificale Romanum*.

and was probably written by the early Reformers. There is also a free popular translation made by John Dryden in 1687—

> "Creator Spirit, by whose aid
> The world's foundations first were laid."
> *(Hymnal Comp. 248)*

and another by Edward Caswall—

> "Come, Holy Ghost, Creator blest,
> Vouchsafe within our souls to rest."
> *(Ancient & Mod. 347)*

We must now turn to the two contemporary Bernards, Bernard of Clairvaux and Bernard of Clugny. Bernard, the Abbot of Clairvaux, or the great Bernard, was born at Fontaine in Burgundy, in 1091. To him we owe the following:—

> "Jesu, the very thought of Thee
> With sweetness fills the breast."
> *(Ancient & Mod. 178; Hymnal Comp. 287)*

a translation by Edward Caswall;

> "Jesu, the very thought is sweet,
> In that dear Name all heart-joys meet."
> *(Ancient & Mod. 177; Church Hymns 402; Hymnal Comp. 286)*

translated by J. M. Neale; and—

> "Jesu, Thou joy of loving hearts,
> Thou Fount of life, Thou Light of men."
> *(Ancient & Mod. 190; Church Hymns 403; Hymnal Comp. 376)*

an excellent translation by the American, Dr Ray Palmer.[1]

These are all from portions of the one metrical Latin poem, nearly 200 lines long, generally known as—

>Jesu, dulcis memoria[2],

from its first line.

From another of Bernard's pieces—

>Salve Caput cruentatum,

is translated, by Sir Henry Baker—

>"O sacred Head, surrounded
>By crown of piercing thorn!"
>(*Ancient & Mod.* 111)[3]

---

[1] Dr Ray Palmer is also the author of the hymns—

>"Jesu, these eyes have never seen."
>(*Hymnal Comp.* 288)

and—

>"My faith looks up to thee."
>(*Hymnal Comp.* 266)

[2] It is entitled *Jubilus Rhythmicus, In Commemorationem Dominicæ Passionis* (or *De Nomine Jesu*). From the same are translated—

>"Jesu, thy mercies are untold."
>(*Ancient & Mod.* 189)

>"O Jesu, King most wonderful."
>(*Ancient & Mod.* 178. Part 2)

and—

>"O Jesu, Thou the Beauty art."
>(*Ancient & Mod.* 178. Part 3)

all by Edward Caswall.

[3] The version beginning—

>"O sacred Head, once wounded."
>(*Hymnal Comp.* 172)

is by J. W. Alexander (1849), and is really taken from the famous

This is part of a poem, 370 lines in length, addressed to the members of the body of Christ hanging upon the Cross[1].

I must leave you to study the very interesting life of this Bernard, of one who had perhaps a wider *personal* influence than any man on the roll of European history. The Kings of France and of England, the Emperor of Germany and the Pope were really guided and inspired by him[2]; and his persuasive eloquence ruled the fortunes of Europe. Born of a noble family, at the age of twenty-two he joined the then new monastery of Citeaux in Burgundy, belonging to the great Cistercian order. But the practical founder of that order was Bernard; as Luther called him, "the best monk that

---

German translation made by the poet Gerhardt, who died in 1676—
    O Haupt voll blut und wunden.
and that beginning—
   "Hail that Head, all torn and wounded."
    (*Church Hymns* 377)
is an altered form of a translation by Dean Alford.

[1] It begins—
    Salve, mundi salutare,
    Salve, salve, Jesu care!
and has the title, in some editions, *Rhythmica oratio ad unum quodlibet membrorum Christi patientis, et a cruce pendentis*. The hymn is taken from the last of the seven portions—"*Ad Faciem*"; the first portion is—"*Ad Pedes.*"

[2] Lewis (vi) the Fat; Henry I.; the Emperor Lothair, and Pope Innocent II.

ever lived[1]." Within three years, through his influence, Citeaux was full to overflowing; and Bernard led out the first colony to a barren and desolate valley in Champagne, called the Valley of Wormwood, notorious as a den of robbers. Bernard changed its name to *Clara Vallis*, Clairvaux, the Bright Valley. Such they soon made it. No offers of grandeur or of high office could draw him away. His followers took the dignities. He died in 1153, the humble abbot, the intellectual master of his age, "ascending," says the old chronicler, "from the Bright Valley to the mountain of eternal brightness[2]."

The other Bernard, Bernard of Clugny, is sometimes called "of Morlaix," from Morlaix in Brittany where he was born, although of English parents. He lived and died a monk of the magnificent abbey of Clugny in Auvergne; and dedicated his famous poem to Peter the Venerable, the abbot and general of his order, and himself a distinguished poet. This poem, about 3000 lines in length, is entitled "On Contempt of the

---

[1] The true founder of the order was Stephen Harding, an Englishman. Luther's remarks on Bernard were not entirely complimentary, e.g. "the best monk that ever lived, whom I love beyond all the rest put together; yet he dared to say, it were a sign of damnation if a man quitted his monastery."—*Table Talk*.

[2] Compare Milman, *Latin Christianity*, Book viii. Chap. 4; Robertson, *Christian Church*, Book vi. Chap. 8.

World," but begins with a description of the second coming of Christ and the glory of heaven—

Hora novissima, tempora pessima sunt, vigilemus.

A translation of part of this poem, 442 lines in length, was made by Dr Neale, and published under the title—*The Rhythm of Bernard de Morlaix*[1].

The hold it has got on the affections of Christian people is manifest when we know that from this translation are taken these familiar hymns—

Hic breve vivitur, hic breve plangitur, hic breve fletur,
"Brief life is here our portion."
(Ancient & Mod. 226; Church Hymns 341; Hymnal Comp. 239)

O bona patria, lumina sobriate speculantur,
"For thee, O dear, dear country."
(Ancient & Mod. 227; Church Hymns 365; Hymnal Comp. 239)

---

[1] In 1859; also published in *Mediæval Hymns and Sequences*, 3rd edition, p. 71. Dr Neale confesses that he was obliged to deviate from his ordinary rule of adopting the measure of the original. So difficult was the Latin metre, that Bernard in his introduction expresses his belief that nothing but the special grace of God could have enabled him to use it throughout so long a poem. The difficulty will be seen when it is noted, that the poem is written in dactylic hexameters, each line divided into three equal parts. Moreover, they unite the leonine or internal rhyme and the tailed rhyme; the former between the two first clauses of each line, the latter between the two consecutive lines. The second and two following lines of the poem will serve as examples—

Ecce! minaciter imminet arbiter ille supremus.
Imminet, imminet, ut mala terminet, æqua coronet,
Recta remuneret, anxia liberet, æthera donet.

and—
>   Urbs Syon aurea, patria lactea, cive decora,
>   "Jerusalem the golden."
>   *(Ancient & Mod. 228; Church Hymns 395; Hymnal Comp. 239)*

Another from the same source is—
>   "The world is very evil,
>   The times are waxing late."
>   *(Ancient & Mod. 226)*

There is a touching little story, told with some just pride by Dr Neale, of a child who was ill and in great suffering. The medical attendants could do but little to ease its agonies of pain. But the child would lie without a murmur and almost without motion while the whole of those four hundred lines on the better country were being read to it.

We cannot dwell upon the hymns of Adam of S. Victor, Bonaventura and others who lived at the end of the 12th and the beginning of the 13th centuries. The former, called S. Victor from the Abbey of S. Victor near Paris, is spoken of by Archbishop Trench as "the greatest of the Latin hymnologists of the middle ages[1]."

---

[1] *Sacred Latin Poetry*, p. 53. "The greatest of mediæval poets," says Dr Neale. Among his hymns is the one for S. Stephen's day—
>   Heri mundus exultavit,
>   "Yesterday with exultation."
>   *(Ancient & Mod. 64)*

See also Appendix, page 238.

Of Bonaventura, otherwise Giovani di Fidenza—the "Seraphic Doctor," the theological opponent of Thomas Aquinas—the best known is his Passion hymn[1]. He it was who, when asked from what books he had gained his great wisdom, pointed to his crucifix, the representation of Christ upon the Cross. Few of their hymns appear in our hymn-books.

Before we conclude, I must refer to two most celebrated hymns, one the *Stabat Mater dolorosa*, which has been wedded by Rossini to such exquisite music. It appears in the version—

> "At the Cross, her station keeping,
> Stood the mournful Mother weeping."
> *(Ancient & Mod.* 117)

an altered form of Bishop Mant's translation[2].

---

[1] The Passion hymn of Bonaventura—

> In Passione Domini
> Qua datur salus homini

is translated by Rev. Frederick Oakeley—

> "In the Lord's atoning grief."
> *(Ancient & Mod.* 105)

[2] Bishop Mant's translation (see page 180) begins—

> "By the Cross sad vigil keeping."

The first verse of the Latin hymn is—

> Stabat Mater dolorosa
> Juxta crucem lachrymosa,
> Dum pendebat Filius;
> Cujus animam gementem,
> Contristantem et dolentem
> Pertransivit gladius.

The Dies Iræ.

The *Stabat Mater* was written at the end of the 13th century by Jacobus de Benedictis, or more familiarly Jacopone da Todi, so called from Todi of Umbria, in Italy, where he was born. He was of noble family, a lawyer; but the sudden death of his wife by an accident led him to become a lay brother of the order of S. Francis. By his rough humorous rhymes, he did very much to reform the religious abuses of his day. He wrote hymns in Latin and Italian, some of which, we are told, were of no little comfort to him when his own last hours drew on.

The other hymn is the famous *Dies Iræ*, "Day of Wrath," written by Thomas of Celano, in the Abruzzi in Italy, the friend and biographer of Francis of Assisi, in the 13th century. No Latin hymn is so famous as this. How many authors and translators has it inspired!

"Day of wrath! O day of mourning!
See once more the Cross returning."
(*Ancient & Mod.* 398; *Church Hymns* 355; *Hymnal Comp.* 68)

a fine translation by Dr W. J. Irons, published in 1848. A translation by Sir Walter Scott is introduced by him with much effect at the close of *The Lay of the Last Minstrel*, at the requiem in the Abbey of Melrose:—

"Then mass was sung, and prayers were said,
And solemn requiem for the dead;
And bells toll'd out their mighty peal,
For the departed spirit's weal;

>   And ever in the office close
>   The hymn of intercession rose ;
>   And far the echoing aisles prolong
>   The awful burthen of the song—
>   DIES IRÆ, DIES ILLA,
>   SOLVET SÆCLUM IN FAVILLA ;
>   While the pealing organ rung ;
>   Were it meet with sacred strain
>   To close my lay, so light and vain,
>   Thus the holy fathers sung :—
>   HYMN FOR THE DEAD.
>   That day of wrath, that dreadful day,
>   When heaven and earth shall pass away."
>   .   .   .   .
>   (*Ancient & Mod.* 206; *Hymnal Comp.* 63)

And there is a translation by John Newton—

> "Day of judgment, day of wonders,
> Hark, the trumpet's awful sound."
>   (*Hymnal Comp.* 65)

The *Dies Iræ* appears in the *Sarum Missal* among the "Memorials for the dead," and is headed 'A Prose for the Departed.'

The great German writer Goethe has also introduced the hymn into his wonderful play of Faust, in the Cathedral scene at the end of the first part. The hymn has found expression in the grand music of Mozart. Dr Johnson loved to quote it in his most solemn moments. With Sir Walter Scott, it was ever a special favourite; and we learn, that in his last days, when his great mind was failing fast, he was often heard to murmur some of the words of this sublime hymn—

"Be THOU the trembling sinner's stay,
Tho' heaven and earth shall pass away[1]."

I venture to hope that our consideration of these hymns may, perhaps, lead us to think a little more of the words as we sing them.

And in conclusion I will point my moral with a tale, a mediæval tale, which I first saw quoted by the

---

[1] The effect of the peculiar metre and of the triple rhyme in the Latin hymn "has been likened to blow following blow of the hammer on the anvil" (Trench, *Sacred Latin Poetry*). A few lines are quoted—except the third line, those quoted by Goethe—

Dies iræ, dies illa
Solvet sæclum in favilla
Teste David cum Sibylla.
. . . . .
. . . . .
Judex ergo quum sedebit,
Quidquid latet apparebit,
Nil inultum remanebit.
Quid sum miser tum dicturus,
Quem patronum rogaturus,
Quum vix justus sit securus?

Instead of the third line, there is in the *Paris Breviary* and elsewhere the line—

Crucis expandens vexilla,

in reference to S. Matt. xxiv. 30. Compare the Vulgate Version of Zephaniah i. 15—Dies iræ, dies illa, dies tribulationis et angustiæ, *et seq.*

Rev. Samuel John Stone, the author of the hymn—

·"The Church's one foundation[1]
Is Jesus Christ her Lord."

(Ancient & Mod. 215; Church Hymns 509; Hymnal Comp. 285)

It is found in a book of poems entitled *Legenda Monastica*, and is called "Brother Wilfrith's Story." It tells us, how seven holy men resolved to dedicate their lives to God, and took for their chapel a lovely forest glade. One grief they had; they were old and not musical. Their abbot, therefore, gave them leave simply to say, instead of singing, their chants and hymns. God would accept it, if they brought the best they had to bring. But he positively excepted the *Magnificat*, which they were directed to try and chant as best they could. "So," goes on the poem—

"So every day, at Vesper time, Magnificat was heard.
'Tis said, that from the boughs above, it frightened every bird,
For all were out of tune, and each a different chant did try;
But up in heaven, where hearts are known, it made sweet melody."

---

[1] Also of—

"Weary of earth and laden with my sin."
(Ancient & Mod. 252; Church Hymns 544; Hymnal Comp. 149)

These both appeared in his *Lyra Fidelium, twelve hymns on the Twelve Articles of the Apostles' Creed*, 1865.

And the Missionary hymn—

"Through midnight gloom from Macedon."
(Ancient & Mod. 361)

One Christmas Eve a young stranger joined them, to whose exquisite singing they listened in amaze:—

"And each one in his heart exclaimed, 'Thank God that
   on this night
 One is among us who can sing Magnificat aright.'
 But had they marked the stranger's face, and seen how
   all his thought
 Was on his own melodious voice—how *self* was all he
   sought—
 They would have known, that up in heaven that voice
   was never heard;
 For though the *birds* came flying back, CHRIST could not
   hear a word."

At the close of their service, an angel appeared demanding why no praise had been offered "on that night so blest." Thereupon, in much fear, they bade depart that melodious stranger:—

"Then bursting forth into the chants, it was their wont to
   sing,
 High up in heaven, their hymn of praise, with fervent
   heart they fling.
 And the angel bare it on with him, to heaven's Lord
   and King."

LECTURE II.

THE REFORMATION PERIOD.

LECTURE II.

IN our last Lecture we avoided any definition of a "hymn." We deferred our consideration of the word. The time has now come when some more restricted meaning of the terms "psalm" and "hymn" has become necessary. The word "hymn" is essentially a Greek, and not a Latin, word. Among the Greeks, a hymn was a song or poem, often in honour of some famous person, often on occasions of war or of marriage. It was generally in metre, and was said to be "hymned." I will mention but one—the hymn to Zeus of the Greek poet, Cleanthes, about 300 B.C.[1] From this, Aratus took the words which his more famous fellow-countryman, the scholar and Apostle Paul of Tarsus, addressed to the men of Athens—"For we are also his offspring[2]."

---

[1] See the account s. v. in the *Dictionary of Greek and Roman Biography*.

[2] In the *Exordium* of the *Phænomena*—
"Jove fills the heaven, the earth, the sea, the air;
We feel his spirit moving everywhere;
And we his offspring are."
See also Acts xvii. 28.

We turn to the Septuagint or Greek Version of the Old Testament, and we find that the Psalms are there also called "hymns"; for instance, "the hymns (in the Authorized Version 'prayers') of the son of Jesse are ended" (Ps. lxxii. 20). From the Septuagint we also get the word "Psalms," as used in the Christian Church. In the original Hebrew they are called *Tehillim*, "Praises," "Songs of Praise." A "psalm" implied a musical accompaniment, such as a psaltery or other stringed instrument, from *psallo* (ψάλλω), to touch or pull. The "hymn" has now a very wide range, and includes the "psalm[1]." Augustine gave a definition which was long accepted in the ancient days of the Church—"Hymns are songs containing the praise of God[2]." But we have seen that they very early contained prayer and meditation as well as praise. And such are their characteristics in modern times. Some-

---

[1] When S. Paul distinguished "psalms and hymns and spiritual songs," or "odes" (Ephes. v. 19; Col. iii. 16), he probably referred "psalms" to the Psalms of David, "hymns" to songs of praise which were essentially of a *Christian* character, and the "songs" or "odes," the general word for songs, to all kinds of songs and including the two former—only they were to be "spiritual"; see also p. 6.

[2] "Hymni laudes sunt Dei cum cantico, hymni cantus sunt continentes laudem Dei. Si sit laus, et non sit Dei, non est hymnus; si sit laus, et Dei laus, et non cantetur, non est hymnus. Oportet, ergo, ut, si sit hymnus, habeat hæc tria, et laudem, et Dei, et canticum."—Augustine, *Enarr. in Ps. lxxii.* Lat.

times, hymns had merely rhythm, like the *Te Deum*, or any of the Psalms, or one of the mediæval sequences. At others, they had metre, and were in verse; and at a later period, they began to be in rhyme.

At first, the known Christian poets, both of the Greek and Latin Church, wrote in the classical metres[1]. By degrees, these classical metres were found to be unsuited for popular Church use; and after the sixth century *quantity* in syllables gave way to accent, as in the verse of modern languages. Then, in the West, rhyme was introduced, at first fitfully, until among the hymn writers of the 11th and 12th centuries, rhyme was generally adopted.

What we have to deal with are nearly all rhymed and metrical hymns.

"The Reformation period" covers a wide field. It is hard to say when the Reformation began. It grew from small beginnings, a necessity in men's minds. Hymns played a by no means unimportant part in

---

[1] Thus Gregory Nazianzen, bishop A.D. 370, used the ordinary Greek metres. In the West, Ambrose and his followers adopted the most rhythmical metre, the Iambic Dimeter, similar to our Long Measure; and rhymes occasionally appear among the earlier Latin hymn poets—even so early as Hilary of Poitiers (A.D. 354) in his Epiphany hymn—
Jesus refulsit omnium.
In the East, beginning with Anatolius in the 5th century, verse made way for rhythmical prose, and it had vanished by the 8th century, while here rhyme was never developed.

bringing it about. Some of the hymns of the later Roman Church had asserted her peculiar doctrines with equal boldness and power. We may instance the hymns of Thomas Aquinas, of Aquino in Naples, in the 13th century, the "Angelic Doctor" as he was called, the greatest of the Schoolmen. Five of these hymns set out the Roman doctrine of Transubstantiation with great force and accuracy, and are said to have done no little to secure its after prevalence. They were written for the Festival of Corpus Christi, which Aquinas induced Pope Urban IV. to institute in 1264. Translations of some of these, of course much changed in substance from the originals, are given in our Hymnals:—

> Pange lingua gloriosi Corporis mysterium,
> "Now, my tongue, the mystery telling
> Of the glorious Body sing."
> *(Ancient & Mod. 309)*

translated by the Compilers of *Hymns Ancient and Modern*.

> Adoro Te devote, latens Deitas,
> "Thee we adore, O hidden Saviour, Thee."
> *(Ancient & Mod. 312; Church Hymns 216)*

translated by Bishop Woodford, the late Bishop of Ely[1].

---

[1] He is also the author of the Christmas hymn—

> "God from on high hath heard,"
> *(Ancient & Mod. 58; Church Hymns 79)*

founded on a Latin hymn by Charles Coffin in the *Paris Breviary*—

> Jam desinant suspiria.

This was never, says Dr Neale, in public use in the mediæval Church[1]. It is fairly open to question whether these, although, as I said, much changed and adapted, are wisely inserted in our Church Hymnals. It would seem to be unnecessary to go to such a source with so many hundreds of beautiful hymns of all kinds

---

[1] The others are—
> Verbum supernum prodiens,
> Nec Patris linquens dexteram,
> "The heavenly Word proceeding forth."
> (*Ancient & Mod.* 311)

translated by J. M. Neale, but altered. It should be noted that there is an Ambrosian Latin hymn with the same first line, translated by the Compilers of *Hymns Ancient and Modern*, No. 46—
> "O heavenly Word, eternal Light."

Then—
> Ecce panis angelorum,
> "Lo, the angels' Food is given."
> (*Ancient & Mod.* 310)

a translation by Sir H. Baker of the last two verses of, perhaps, the most famous, beginning—
> Lauda Sion Salvatorem.

This it would be impossible to adapt to a Church of England version. Mendelssohn's Cantata, *Lauda Sion*, was written for a Roman Catholic festival at Liège in 1846.

The fifth hymn for the Festival of Corpus Christi, which was held on the Thursday after the Octave of Pentecost, was—
> Sacris solemniis juncta sint gaudia,
> "Let this our solemn Feast
> With holy joys be crowned,"

a translation by J. D. Chambers given in his *Sarum Psalter*. The Latin hymns are in Daniel, *Thesaurus Hymnol.* i. 251; ii. 97.

at our disposal. We may, perhaps, echo the hope expressed by Bishop Alexander, "that our hymn writers will not sail too near the wind, whether towards the coast of Italy, or in the opposite direction of Plymouth Sound."

We must not run away with the too common opinion, that the Service Books in the unreformed Church of England contained only hymns which were doctrinally objectionable. The great majority were not so. It is capable of clear proof that in this Cathedral of Carlisle, just before the Reformation, the Sarum Breviary and Missal were used, and not those of York, or Hereford, or any other Use. Among the hymns of the Sarum Breviary, which were sung at the daily Hours of Prayer, were very many of those beautiful ancient hymns which we considered in our last Lecture[1]. There are two, not indeed in the ordinary Sarum Breviary, but which had a very wide use—

> Alleluia, dulce carmen,
> "Alleluia, song of sweetness,
> Voice of joy that cannot die."
> *(Ancient & Mod. 82; Church Hymns 102; Hymnal Comp. 530)*

---

[1] The beautiful hymn sung at Compline—
> Salvator mundi, Domine.

seems to be peculiar to the English Service Books. A translation by J. W. Copeland (altered) is—
> "O Saviour Lord, to Thee we pray."
> *(Ancient & Mod. 63)*

The Latin hymn, whose author is unknown, is, at the latest, of the 9th century; the translation is founded on one made by J. M. Neale[1].

The other, the *Alleluia Perenne*, so called from its refrain—"An endless Alleluia"—is also by an unknown author, and is probably older than the 9th century. The hymn begins—

> Alleluia piis edite laudibus,
> "Sing Alleluia forth in duteous praise."
> (*Ancient & Mod.* 296; *Church Hymns* 497; *Hymnal Comp.* 494)

and is found in the very ancient Mozarabic or Spanish Breviary[2]. The translation is by the Rev. John Ellerton.

With such as these, the members of the Roman Church were not contented. When they revised their Breviary, they reformed the whole body of their hymns, commencing the work under Pope Leo X. A volume of new

---

[1] The hymn is placed by Dr Neale not earlier than the 13th century; but both this and the *Alleluia Perenne* are found in Anglo-Saxon Hymnaries of the 10th and 11th centuries. It is there given to be sung on the Saturday before Septuagesima Sunday. They are also both in the *Worcester Breviary* (Chambers).

[2] It is there given to be sung at Vespers on the first Sunday in Lent. As a general rule, in the Latin Church, at all events after the 6th century, the use of *Alleluia* was intermitted between Septuagesima and Easter. But this rule varied in the Mozarabic rite, which in many respects was similar to that of the Eastern Churches. In the *Worcester Breviary* this hymn is given to be sung in Septuagesima. Compare also Daniel *Thesaurus Hymnol.* iv. 64.

hymns was published in 1523. Recourse was had once more to the old classical Latin metres. This work of revision was completed under Pope Urban VIII. in 1631, before the last revision of our Prayer-Book in 1662. Many of the ancient hymns were expunged; others were altered so that they could scarcely be recognized. Thus the Hymnary was produced which is in general use in Roman Catholic churches throughout the world[1].

It is strange that the compilers of our Prayer-Book did not at the first retain the equally beautiful hymns, as well as so many of the prayers, of the old Service Books of the Church of England. It was the wish of Archbishop Cranmer, that, as had been done in Germany, they should in England keep the best of the hymns of the ancient Church. In King Henry VIII.'s Primer, ordered in 1545 to be used throughout the kingdom, there are English metrical translations of some of the more noted ancient hymns. But with the First Prayer-Book of Edward VI. in 1549, there fell a darkness upon the hymnody of the public worship of the Church of England which lasted for nigh 300 years. The causes which brought this about, we shall note later on. We must now go to Germany, and see what had been done there.

---

[1] In some Roman Catholic churches, other hymnaries are also in use. On the hymns introduced at a later period into the *Paris Breviary*, see below, p. 124.

Martin Luther.

A great name at once meets us, not simply of a reformer, but of a musician and a poet, Martin Luther, born in 1483 at the village of Eisleben in Saxony. "In the history of the Reformation," says Hallam, "incomparably the greatest name." We cannot enter on the details of his life, but must just sketch the incidents which bear upon his hymns. His father was a poor miner. The young boy, as children often did in those times, sang for alms in the public streets. At the age of eighteen, he entered the University of Erfurt. There intended for the law, he greatly distinguished himself. He devoted himself much to literature and music. But soon he began to be troubled with religious doubts and scruples. Despite the dissuasions of his father and others, he entered the Augustine Convent at Erfurt. "Of a truth, I was a pious monk," he says: "if ever a monk got to heaven by monkery, I was determined to get there." Still, it was an aged monk, John von Staupitz, the Vicar-General of his Order, who comforted his distress of mind, who taught him that Christ was the atonement for all sins, *and* that this was declared in the Apostles' Creed. It was in the Convent Library that he found the copy of the Scriptures, which had such an effect on him and on the Christian world[1].

---

[1] This finding of the Bible has been much disputed; but most of Luther's German biographers agree, that it was in the convent the Vulgate first came into his hands as a book to be

Familiar to all must be his appointment as professor at the new University of Wittenberg, his visit to Rome and the shock it gave him, his long contest with the emissaries of the Papal power, and then his bold act of defiance, the burning of the Papal bull of condemnation, in December 1520, at the Elster gate of Wittenberg[1]. The great concourse of people looked on and shouted. "The Pope," says Thomas Carlyle, "should not have provoked that shout. It was the shout of the awakening of nations[2]."

All through his life, Luther was intensely fond of music and of poetry. The time had come when they were to be mighty powers in his hand. The most celebrated of Luther's hymns was his paraphrase of the 46th Psalm—

>Ein feste Burg ist unser Gott,
>"A sure stronghold our God is He,
>A trusty shield and weapon."

It is believed generally to have been written by Luther when he was on his way to the Diet of Worms in 1521[3]. Thither he had been summoned, by the

---

read. Hagenbach places the incident in the Erfurt University Library.

[1] Compare for this and other incidents, the excellent *Life of Luther* (trans.) by Julius Köstlin.

[2] Carlyle, *Lectures on Heroes*, "The Hero as Priest."

[3] It is said by some to have been composed after the second Diet of Spires in February 1529, when the *protest* was made and the name *Protestant* given; but this can scarcely be the case as it

Emperor Charles V. and the other Princes of the Empire, to appear and answer for himself, whether he would recant or not. His friends tried to dissuade him from going. They reminded him that John Huss was burned to death. To one of them, Spalatin, court preacher to the Elector of Saxony, he wrote thus—"If there were as many devils in Worms as there are tiles on the roofs, I would on, and would not be afraid. If Huss was burned to ashes, the truth was not burned with him[1]." As he went to the Hall of the Diet, the vast crowds called upon him to be firm. He passed on singing this hymn:—

> "A sure stronghold our God is He,
>   A trusty shield and weapon;
> Our help He'll be and set us free
>   From every ill can happen.
> That old malicious foe
> Intends us deadly woe;
> Arm'd with the strength of hell
> And deepest craft as well,
> On earth is not his fellow.

---

appears in a Collection dated 1529. Köstlin places it at the time of the plague at Wittenberg, when Luther used very similar language.

[1] See Hagenbach, *History of the Reformation*, and Miss Winkworth's *Christian Singers of Germany*.

Through our own force we nothing can,
   Straight were we lost for ever;
But for us fights the proper Man,
   By God sent to deliver.
   Ask ye who this may be?
   Christ Jesus named is He,
   Of Sabaoth the Lord;
   Sole God to be adored;
   'Tis He must win the battle.

And were the world with devils fill'd,
   All eager to devour us,
Our souls to fear should little yield,
   They cannot overpower us.
   Their dreaded Prince no more
   Can harm us as of yore;
   Look grim as e'er he may,
   Doom'd is his ancient sway;
   A word can overthrow him[1]."

. . . .
. . . . . .

It was part of Luther's faith that there were devils about continually besetting men. Perhaps, he was right.

---

[1] *Lyra Germanica*, Series i. pp. xviii, 175, a translation by Rev. W. Gaskell. The original, of four stanzas, is given in Bunsen *Gesangbuch*, No. 261.

Hymns of Luther.

Luther also composed the grand tune, or chorale, to this hymn[1], and sang it often afterwards. The hymn was soon a favourite with the people, and went by his name. It became, as Heine called it, "the Marseillaise of the Reformation." It has cheered on armies to the battle. It has lived in the hearts of the German nation. Its first line is cut on Luther's tomb at Wittenberg; "and by it, he, being dead, yet speaketh."

From this time of trial onward, Luther worked earnestly at Church music and hymns. He knew what a powerful instrument they would prove. He gathered his musical friends together, his "house-choir," as he called them, to help him in the selection of suitable and popular tunes. He himself wrote thirty-six hymns, some of them translations from the old Latin originals, which *he* counted as among the good things which God's power had kept alive. Successive hymn books were compiled and put forth. The first published was the *Erfurter Enchiridion* or *Handbook* in 1524[2], "the year," as it has been said, "in which German hymnody was born." Luther himself taught the people

---

[1] It is the tune to which generally is taken Sir Henry Baker's hymn —
   "Rejoice to-day with one accord."
See page 253.

[2] Luther had put out a small volume of eight hymns early in the same year, 1524 (Köstlin).

to sing from them. The result was astounding. Hymns printed too on single sheets, with tunes, were carried over Germany by wandering students and pedlars. They were sung everywhere—in the fields, the streets, the workshops, the cottages, as well as in the Churches. 'The whole people," wrote a Romanist at the time, 'is singing itself into this Lutheran doctrine." "Luther did as much," said Coleridge, "for the Reformation by his hymns as by his translation of the Bible." Anyhow, they had a marvellous effect upon Christian worship in the land, and gave it that noble congregational character which it has never lost.

Two more of his hymns must be noticed, though scarcely well adapted to our Services. One, perhaps the most popular at that day, is a remarkable epitome of the doctrine of salvation through Christ :—

> Nun freut euch, lieben Christen gemein,
>
> "Dear Christian people, now rejoice,
> Our hearts within us leap."

Its tune is that which we know so well, and use to what is often called "Luther's hymn"—but which, we shall see, is not Luther's—

> "Great God, what do I see and hear?"

Luther is said to have noted the tune down as he heard a travelling artizan singing it. "Many hundred Christians," says a writer of the time, "have been brought to the true faith by that one hymn alone[1]." The didactic character of this and of many of the hymns of that period has prevented their introduction into general public worship. After Luther's death, there was an assembly at Frankfurt, in 1557, of many of the Princes who had embraced the reformed religion. They wished to have an Evangelical service in one of the churches. A great congregation came together. But a Roman Catholic priest occupied the pulpit, and improved the occasion. They listened for a time in silence. Then the immense body of people rose to their feet; and they one and all burst forth into this hymn with the magnificent roll of its grand tune. Before they had finished, the preacher had gone.

The other hymn—

Aus tiefer Noth schrei ich zu Dir,
"Out of the depths I cry to Thee,"

was composed by Luther in 1524, in the very midst of his contest and his troubles. Later, during the Diet of Augsburg in 1530, he was one day so overcome with what he had gone through, that he fainted. On recovering, he said to his friends, "Come let us defy the devil and praise God by singing the hymn—Out of the

---

[1] Compare Miss Winkworth's *Christian Singers of Germany*, p. 112, who gives a translation of the hymn, and to whom I am indebted here. See also Koch, *Geschichte des Kirchenlieds*, vol. viii. p. 4.

depths I cry to Thee." It is said to have been the last Protestant hymn sung in Strasburg Cathedral. It has ever been one of the funeral hymns of Germany; and it was sung by the vast concourse who, in 1546, attended the body of Luther to the grave[1].

A truly great man and a good man; at times bold and rough, but withal tender and loving as a child. I part, with regret, from—"the monk who shook the world."

The history of the darkness which so long brooded over English hymnody is not a little curious. One would have thought that the light, which had shone in Germany, would have appeared and been followed in this country. The darkness spread hither from France

---

[1] Another hymn should be mentioned, the Christmas hymn, or carol, written by Luther for his little son Hans in 1535—

Vom Himmel hoch da komm ich her,
"From heaven above to earth I come,"

translated by Miss Winkworth in *Lyra Germanica* (i. 12). Part of it is given as a hymn in the *Hymnal Companion*, beginning—

"Give heed, my heart, lift up thine eyes."
(*Hymnal Comp.* 415)

Also the Easter hymn—

Christ lag in Todesbanden,
"Christ Jesus lay in Death's strong bands,"
(*Church Hymns* 129)

translated by Richard Massie.

and Geneva. A metrical translation of part of the Psalms was made about 1540 by Clément Marot, groom of the chambers to the French King, Francis I. He dedicated his work to the King, and 'Aux Dames de France.' Being set to popular airs, these psalms became very fashionable, alike in the court and among the people[1]. Before this, Marot had got into disgrace at court, turned Calvinist, and gone to Geneva. The atmosphere of Geneva did not suit the gay poet. He went back *to* his country, and *from* Calvinism. But he had once more to flee from France, and he died at Turin

---

[1] Marot published fifty-two Psalms "traduitz en rithm Francais selon la verité Hébraique." There is a strange account of the rage for these Psalms which took possession of the French court, in D'Israeli's *Curiosities of Literature*, under the heading "Psalm-singing." Marot anticipated in his Preface what Calvin carried out—

>"O bien heureux qui voir pourra
>Fleurir le temps, que l'on orra
>Le laboreur à sa charrue,
>Le charretier parmy la rue,
>Et l'artisan en sa boutique
>Avecques un PSEAUME ou cantique,
>En son labeur se soulager;
>Heureux qui orra le berger
>Et la bergere en bois estans
>Faire que rochers et estangs
>Après eux chantent la hauteur
>Du saint nom de leur Createur.
>>Commences, dames, commencez
>>Le siècle doré! avancez!
>>En chantant d'un cueur debonnaire
>>Dedans ce saint cancionnaire."

in 1544. His *Psalms*, however, lived, in Geneva as well as in France. For about this time, Calvin, having returned from exile in 1541, was organizing the reformed Church of Geneva. He feared, as he said, that in a religious service limited to prayer and preaching only, the congregation would remain cold and inattentive. He felt that music and singing were a power to be used on the side of the Reformation. But he had got the unfortunate belief, already condemned in the ancient Church[1], that everything sung in Divine worship must be taken directly from the Scriptures. Marot's *Psalms*, completed by the famous Theodore Beza, with a simple musical notation, came in opportunely. They were adopted; and a music master, who was paid by the State, gave three lessons a week to several choirs of children. The system grew; and Marot's *Psalms* for centuries enslaved the Protestants of Switzerland and France[2].

About the same period, there was in England another groom of the robes, groom to King Henry VIII., and afterwards to Edward VI.—Thomas Sternhold. He was a native of Hampshire, educated at Oxford; and he

---

[1] At the fourth council of Toledo, A.D. 633, when Isidore of Seville presided. Doubts on the subject having arisen in the Church, the use of other hymns, in addition to the Ambrosian hymns, was formally sanctioned by the second Council of Tours, A.D. 567.

[2] Compare Guizot's *S. Louis and Calvin*, p. 264.

also made a metrical translation of a portion of the Psalms. A zealous reformer, Sternhold was anxious to do away with the improper songs used about the Court. I am afraid he was not successful. Little more is known of him. Thirty-seven of these psalms were published just about the time of his death in 1549[1]. Another edition was put out in 1551 with seven psalms by John Hopkins, who had taken a degree at Oxford and became a clergyman in Suffolk. During Queen Mary's reign, the English refugees at Geneva made some additions. Their first Service Book, published in 1556, contained fifty-one psalms[2]. On their return, when Elizabeth came to the throne, this Version was brought into general use. The first complete edition of this, "The Old Version," was published in 1562[3]; and, we observe,

---

[1] He had completed translating fifty-one of the Psalms. The title of the book was—'All such Psalm of David as Thomas Sternholde did in his Lyfe drawe into English Metre,' London, 1549.

[2] Of these, forty-four were by Sternhold or by Hopkins, with seven others added.

[3] This was published in London by John Daye under the title—'The whole Booke of *Psalmes*, Collected into English Meeter, by T. Sternhold, I. Hopkins and others, conferred with the Ebrue, with apt Notes to sing them withal.' The title page also stated that they were—"Set forth and allowed to be sung in all churches of all the people before and after Morning and Evening Prayer, as also before and after Sermons, and moreover in private houses for their godly solace and comfort laying apart all ungodly songs and ballads, which tend only to the nourishing

one or two hymns and metrical paraphrases, despite Geneva, were placed at the end[1].

This Old Version was "allowed to be sung of the people in the Churches;" although by what exact authority is not quite clear. It became an incubus on the Church. Some of us have heard it even in this generation. May it rest in peace! "They were men," says Thomas Fuller, "whose piety was better than their poetry." "The Version," says James Montgomery, "is supposed to adhere well to the original; but it is the resemblance of the dead to the living[2]." Let us take one or two examples—examples that do not touch on Sacred Names:—

---

of vice and corrupting of youth." It was hence often called *Daye's Psalter*. It contained forty by Sternhold, and sixty-seven by Hopkins. Among the "other" authors were William Whittingham, afterwards Dean of Durham, William Kethe, and John Mardley.

[1] Among them the "Humble Lamentation of a Sinner," see page 222.

[2] So great was the passion for versifying at this period, that we find such works as these:—'The Actes of the Apostles, translated into Englyshe Metre and dedicated to the Kynge's moste excellent Majestye, by Cristofer Tye, Doctor in Musyke and one of the Gentylmen of his Grace's most honourable Chappell; wyth notes to eche Chapter, to synge and also to playe upon the Lute, very necessary for Studentes after theyr studye to fyle theyr wyttes, and also for all Christians that cannot synge to read the good and godlie storyes of the Liues of Christ Hys Apostles.' 1553.

Ps. vii. 16, "He digs a ditch, and delves it deep,
　　　　　in hope to hurt his brother;
　　　　But he shall fall into the pit
　　　　　that he dig'd up for other."

Ps. xvi. 3, "They shall heape sorrow on their heads,
　　　　　which run as they were mad,
　　　　To offer to the idoll-gods.
　　　　　alas, it is too bad."

Ps. xxii. 12, "So many buls do compasse mee,
　　　　　that be full strong of head.
　　　　Yea, buls so fat, as though they had
　　　　　in Basan field beene fed."

Ps. lxxiii. 2, "Yet like a foole I almost slipt,
　　　　　my feete began to slide:
　　　　And ere I wist euen at a pinch,
　　　　　my steps away gan glide."

On the other hand, it would be difficult to find finer stanzas than these, despite the error in the fifth line—

Ps. xviii. 9, "The Lord descended from above,
　10.　　　and bowed the heavens hie:
　　　　And underneath his feete he cast
　　　　　the darknesse of the skie.
　　　　On Cherubs and on Cherubims
　　　　　full royally he rode
　　　　And on the wings of all the winds
　　　　　came flying all abroade."

One of these metrical psalms stands out preeminent, the grand Old Hundredth—

"All people that on earth do dwell[1]."
(Ancient & Mod. 166; Church Hymns 331; Hymnal Comp. 490)

After much controversy, it seems to have been nearly settled that this was written, not by Sternhold or Hopkins, but by William Kethe, a native of Scotland and one of the refugees with John Knox at Geneva. He was chaplain to the British forces at Havre in 1563, and afterwards a clergyman in Dorset. This version of the Hundredth Psalm first appeared in the Psalter published at Geneva in 1556. The initials W. K. are appended to it in the Scotch Psalter, published in 1564[2].

The now famous tune to which it is sung is set to Beza's version of the 134th Psalm in the French Psalter of Geneva, published in 1554. It was printed in the first edition of the Old Version, and afterwards, in 1604, was adapted to the Hundredth Psalm. Guillaume Franc, a music master in Geneva, appears to have been its composer, though the point has been much disputed.

---

[1] The line—
"We are His *folk*, He doth us feed,"
a more natural version of "we are His people," than "we are His flock", is said to be in a copy of the *English Psalter* dated 1561; but 'flock' is probably only a variant of 'folk'.

[2] Some of the earlier editions have no initials, or they are very uncertain. In the first edition of the Old Version, six other psalms are by Kethe. There is good information as to these Psalters in Major G. A. Crawford's notes to the *Irish Church Hymnal*.

Henceforth, for many years, as might have been expected, the number of good and congregational English hymn writers is but scanty, though it includes some great names. At this period, we owe much to the great hymn poets of Germany. The Advent hymn, known so well under the incorrect title of "Luther's hymn," has a complicated history :—

"Great God, what do I see and hear!
The end of things created."
(Ancient & Mod. 52; *Church Hymns* 375; *Hymnal Comp.* 66)

It is founded upon one published in 1586, by Bartholomäus Ringwaldt, a village pastor in Prussia, born at Frankfurt on the Oder. He produced many other hymns which were elicited by the sufferings of that troubled period. Dr William Bengo Collyer, a popular Congregational minister in London at the beginning of this century, saw a translation of the first verse, made by some unknown person. He composed three additional verses; and this, with various alterations, is the hymn which we possess[1]. The tune

---

[1] Collyer's 4th verse, for which another is generally substituted, is—

"Stay, fancy, stay, and close thy wings,
  Repress thy flight too daring.
One wondrous sight my comfort brings,
  The Judge my nature wearing.
Beneath His Cross, I view the Day
When heaven and earth shall pass away,
  And thus prepare to meet Him."

generally used is, as I have said[1], almost certainly by Luther.

It will not be out of place to speak here of two fine hymns written by Philipp Nicolai, the pastor of the town of Unna in Westphalia. They do not appear in most of our hymn books, but one is well known to all. In 1597, a dreadful pestilence was raging there, and more than 1400 persons were carried off. Nicolai, from his window, could see the funerals passing to the graveyard close by. He was led to dwell much on death and the future life; and, soon after, he published a book of religious meditation. To it were appended the hymns which became so remarkably popular; and he wrote for them two fine chorales, which have been called, respectively, the King and the Queen of Chorales. The words and the tune of one of these hymns have given pleasure to thousands as introduced by Mendelssohn into his oratorio of S. Paul:—

> Wachet auf! ruft uns die Stimme,
> "Sleepers wake, a voice is calling,
> It is the watchman on the walls[2]."

---

[1] See p. 68. Ringwaldt's hymn is in seven verses, beginning—
> Es ist gewisslich an der Zeit,

and bears evident traces of the Latin hymn—" Dies irae, dies illa." Very full information on these German hymns and their authors will be found in Koch, *Geschichte des Kirchenlieds und Kirchengesangs*.

[2]
> Wachet auf! ruft uns die Stimme
> Der Wachter sehr hoch auf der Zinne;
> Wach auf, du Stadt Jerusalem! [A

The other is—
>Wie schön leuchtet der Morgenstern,
>"O Morning Star, how fair and bright
>Thou beamest forth in truth and light."

It speaks of the heavenly Marriage Feast. It has been constantly used at marriages in Germany; and in that land the tune rings out from many a city's chimes[1].

The following is what may be called the wedding verse of the hymn, from Miss Winkworth's translation—

>"Then touch the chords of harp and lute,
> Let no sweet music now be mute,
>   But joyously resounding,
> Tell of the Marriage-feast, the Bride,
> The heavenly Bridegroom at her side,
>   'Mid love and joy abounding;
> Shout for triumph, loudly sing ye,
>   Praises bring ye,
>   Fall before Him,
> King of Kings, let all adore Him."

A translation is given in *Lyra Germanica* (ii. p. 225), beginning—
"Wake, awake for night is flying."

See also *Church Hymns* 538, a translation with the same first line by Rev. Edward Arthur Dayman. This, as well as many of the German hymns mentioned in the text, is to be found in Bunsen's well-known *Allgemeines evangelisches Gesang und Gebetuch*. The title of Nicolai's work was *Freudenspiegel des ewigen Lebens*, 1599.

[1] There is a very free translation by Rev. William Mercer, beginning—
"How bright appears the Morning Star."
(*Hymnal Comp.* 527)

The terrible Thirty Years' War, which ravaged Germany from 1618 to 1648, gave birth to many hymns. It was, in the main, a war of the Protestant against the Roman Catholic Religion. It is impossible for us to conceive the awful suffering and desolation produced during that period, when in many districts four-fifths of the population and more than four-fifths of the property were destroyed. A religious war is ever a cruel war. The Emperor Ferdinand II., with his famous generals, Wallenstein and the atrocious Marshal Tilly, was not behindhand in the cruelties inflicted on the States of the Protestant Confederacy. Then, these States secured the aid of the renowned Gustavus Adolphus of Sweden, the Lion of the North. At the battle of Leipsic, in 1631, he swept back the tide of victory. He had given out to his army the watchword, 'God with us.' Just after the combat, the Hero King wrote down his celebrated battle hymn—

Verzage nicht, O Häuflein klein,

"Fear not, O little flock, the foe,"

to which Johann Altenburg composed the music[1]. These are the last lines—

---

[1] The translation is given in *Lyra Germanica* i. 17. Altenburg was a pastor in Thuringia who composed the chorale to this battle song, and to whom the song has been often attributed. It is now allowed, that the hymn was written down roughly by Gustavus immediately after the battle, and improved by his chaplain Fabricius.

"God is with us, we are His own,
  Our victory cannot fail.
Amen, Lord Jesus, grant our prayer!
Great Captain, now Thine arm make bare;
  Fight for us once again!
So shall Thy saints and martyrs raise
A mighty chorus to Thy praise,
  World without end. Amen."

Gustavus himself had done much to lessen the evils of war. He was esteemed even by his enemies. The king pressed forward in his course of conquest. Now Tilly was defeated. The next year, Gustavus had to meet Wallenstein on the fatal field of Lutzen. He advanced at the head of his soldiers, singing his battle song and Luther's hymn—"A sure stronghold our God is He,"—while his whole army joined in chorus. The great Christian warrior perished in the fight; but it was in the hour of victory, and he knew that, as he had just sung—The Lord of hosts was with him, the God of Jacob was his refuge.

For long years, the miseries of war went on. But all things have an end. And just as the dawn of peace began to break over the land, there was produced what has been called the "Te Deum" of Germany—

>   Nun danket alle Gott,
>   Mit Herzen, Mund und Händen,

"Now thank we all our God,
With hearts and hands and voices."
<small>(Ancient & Mod. 379; Church Hymns 439; Hymnal Comp. 46)</small>

translated by Miss Winkworth.

The hymn and the fine chorale to which it was sung were written by Martin Rinkart, the pastor of his native town of Eilenburg in Saxony. All the losses and troubles which he had experienced in the war only gave point to his grateful expressions toward God—

"Oh may this bounteous God
Through all our life be near us,
With ever joyful hearts
And blessed peace to cheer us;
And keep us in His grace,
And guide us when perplexed,
And free us from all ills
In this world and the next."

It is introduced by Mendelssohn into his *"Lobgesang"* or "Hymn of Praise[1]."

In regard to these chorales or tunes, we have already noted how anxious Luther and those who followed him were, that the music to which they set their hymns should be such that the mass of the people could join.

---

[1] Interesting examples of its use are given in Koch, *Geschichte des Kirchenlieds* viii. 168. The tune generally given in our Hymnals is by Johann Crüger, precentor of S. Nicholas' Church, Berlin, who died in 1662. Compare Ecclesiasticus, li. 22—24, with the first two verses.

Here lay one secret of much of their success. The skill shewed in the composition and adaptation of tunes to the hymns with which they were associated at once rendered the hymns popular. Luther, speaking with enthusiasm of the subject, put it, as usual, somewhat strongly—"Music is a fair gift of God, and near allied to Divinity." And again—"Whosoever is not moved by such art as this, must of a truth be a coarse clod, not worthy to hear such lovely music, but only the waste wild bray of the ancient chanting, and the songs and music of the dogs and the pigs[1]."

---

[1] Quoted in *Christian Singers of Germany*, p. 164. Want of time alone prevented a reference in the Lecture to two German hymn poets of great distinction who also belong to the latter half of the 17th century—Louisa Henrietta, Electress of Brandenburg, and Paul Gerhardt. The Electress Louisa was the daughter of the Prince of Orange, and grand-daughter of the famous Huguenot Admiral Coligny. She endeared herself much to the Prussian people. Her third son was afterwards the first King of Prussia. She did much to encourage hymn writing and singing. She herself wrote four hymns, of which the Easter hymn is very well known—
    Jesus, meine Zuversicht,
   "Jesus, my Redeemer lives."
See *Lyra German.* i. 93. Paul Gerhardt was a Lutheran pastor in Berlin, where his hymns and preaching gave him an immense popularity. He was deprived of his living by the Elector, notwithstanding the friendship of the Electress Louisa. He had besides many troubles, as may be gathered from his hymns; he died in 1676. He is the finest and most poetical of German hymn writers. Many good examples are given in *Lyra Germanica*. The familiar hymn by John Wesley—

[Commit

The scattered hymns, produced by writers of great name in England about this period, are rather beautiful lyric poems than hymns adapted for public singing. Such are the efforts of the saintly George Herbert, at the commencement of the 17th century. Even his well-known lines on "Sunday," beginning—

"O day, most calm, most bright."

are no exception[1]. They are said to have been composed by him, and sung to his lute, on the last Sunday

---

"Commit thou all thy griefs
And ways into His hands,"

is a translation from his—

Befiéhl du deine Wege (Bunsen, No. 311).

There is not, perhaps, a more touching hymn in any language than the one he wrote on the death of his son, the last but one of five children—

Du bist zwar mein und bleibest mein,
"Thou'rt mine, yes, still thou art mine own."
(*Lyra Germ.* ii. p. 123).

See also page 42.

[1] They must not be confounded with his exquisite little piece on "Virtue," beginning—

"Sweet day, so cool, so calm, so bright,
The bridal of the earth and sky."

nor with one of John Mason's *Spiritual Songs* (published 1683)—

"Blest day of God, how calm, how bright."
(*Hymnal Comp.* 194)

John Mason was the Rector of Water Stratford, Buckinghamshire, and died in 1694. To him, Watts and other hymn poets have been much indebted (see pages 197, 203).

of his life. This, however, can scarcely have been the case; but on that day, it appears, he sang to his lute the verse—

> "The Sundays of man's life,
> Threaded together on one string,
> Make bracelets to adorn the wife
> Of the eternal glorious King.
> On Sunday heaven's gate stands ope;
> Blessings are plentiful and rife,
> More plentiful than hope."

and he died, in 1633, at his parish of Bemerton, near Salisbury, for which in three short years he had done so much.

His "Antiphon," as he terms it—

> "Let all the world in every corner sing."
> (*Church Hymns* 411)

is sometimes used for a hymn.

He is the author too of the quotation so applicable here—

> "A Verse may find him who a Sermon flies,
> And turn delight into a sacrifice[1]."

In his poem "The Temple," there is what he entitles "A True Hymn." It is his idea of what a hymn should be. At all events, there could scarcely be truer lines than these which occur in it:—

---

[1] *The Church Porch.* Compare Isaak Walton's *Life of George Herbert.*

> "The fineness which a Hymn or Psalm affords,
> Is, when the soul unto the lines accords."

One beautiful hymn, and linked with others of great beauty, must really have been composed somewhere about this time—

> "Jerusalem, my happy home,
> Name ever dear to me."
> <small>(*Ancient & Mod.* 236; *Church Hymns* 393; *Hymnal Comp.* 230)</small>

It has been the source of much discussion, and has a strange history. As it stands, its author is unknown; and it cannot be referred back earlier than 1801[1]. It had, generally, been connected with the name of David Dickson, the Scotch Covenanter, and with a very similar hymn of his, about the year 1650, beginning—

> "O mother dear, Jerusalem."

But this hymn, as well as Dickson's, turns out to be only an altered and shortened form of another hymn with the same heading—

> "Jerusalem, my happy home,
> When shall I come to thee?"
> <small>(*Church Hymns* 392)</small>

There is a force and a fire about this which places it as the first of, what are called, the "New Jerusalem"

---

[1] Lord Selborne in *The Book of Praise* traces it back to the Collection of Dr Williams and Mr Boden (1801), where it is stated to be from the "*Eckington Collection.*"

hymns. It has been found in a manuscript, in the British Museum[1], which is prior to the year 1616. The hymn is entitled, "*A Song made by F. B. P. to the tune of Diana.*" It is ascribed by a great authority, Mr Sedgwick, supported apparently by Lord Selborne, to Francis Baker, Presbyter or Priest—F. B. P.—a Roman Catholic priest who suffered persecution in Queen Elizabeth's time. A few verses will bear quotation here for their quaint beauty and vigour:—

"Jerusalem, my happy home,
    When shall I come to thee?
When shall my sorrows have an end,
    Thy joys when shall I see?

O happy harbour of the saints!
    O sweet and pleasant soil!
In thee no sorrow may be found,
    No grief, no care, no toil.

. . . .
. . . .

Thy saints are crowned with glory great,
    They see God face to face;
They triumph still, they still rejoice,
    Most happy is their case.

. . . .
. . . .

---

[1] A quarto volume of religious songs, No. 15,225. The hymn consists of 26 verses. See *The Book of Praise*, cviii. note, and Bonar, *The New Jerusalem*, 1852.

> Thy gardens and thy gallant walks
>   Continually are green,
> They grow such sweet and pleasant flowers
>   As nowhere else are seen.
>
> Quite through the streets, with silver sound
>   The flood of Life doth flow;
> Upon whose banks on every side
>   The wood of Life doth grow.
>
> There trees do evermore bear fruit,
>   And evermore do spring;
> There evermore the angels sit,
>   And evermore do sing.
>
> Jerusalem, my happy home,
>   Would God I were in thee!
> Would God my woes were at an end,
>   Thy joys that I might see."

But moreover, the hymn appears to be a very free translation from part of a well-known Latin hymn, by an unknown author, probably of the 8th or 9th century, which I have purposely deferred until now—

> Urbs beata, Jerusalem, dicta pacis visio[1].

It may at once be recognized, since to the same Latin

---

[1] This was changed in the reformed *Roman Breviary* (see page 61) into the, perhaps, better known but very inferior—

   Cœlestis urbs, Jerusalem, beata pacis visio.

The two are compared in Daniel, *Thesaurus Hymnol.* i. 239.

source, and more directly, we owe the beautiful dedication hymns—

> "Blessed city, heavenly Salem,
> Vision dear of peace and love."
>
> (*Ancient & Mod.* 396; *Church Hymns* 338; *Hymnal Comp.* 542, which combines two hymns)

and—

> "Christ is made the sure Foundation,
> Christ the Head and Corner Stone."
>
> (*Ancient & Mod.* 396, Part 2; *Church Hymns* 338, Part 2)

translated by Dr Neale[1].

A free translation by John Chandler of the latter part appears in the hymn—

> "Christ is our Corner Stone,
> On Him alone we build[2]."
>
> (*Ancient & Mod.* 239; *Church Hymns* 344; *Hymnal Comp.* 541)

We must not pass by the famous name of John Milton, though he contributed but little to English hymnody. Milton, at different times, made translations of several of the Psalms, especially about the year 1648. The question of a National Psalter, which should supersede the Old Version of Sternhold and Hopkins, was then being much discussed, even in the Long Parliament[3]. He, not improbably, had this controversy in

---

[1] The translation in *Church Hymns* is by Archbishop Benson.
[2] This begins with the 5th verse—
Angulare fundamentum lapis Christus missus est.
[3] See below, pages 94, 127.

view, and was anxious to assist in its settlement. One Psalm, the 136th, written by Milton long before, in 1624, when he was fifteen years old, has found its way into most of our hymn books—

"Let us with a gladsome mind
Praise the Lord for He is kind."
(*Church Hymns* 414; *Hymnal Comp.* 514)

The refrain is deliberately taken by Sir Henry Baker in his hymn—

"Praise, O praise our God and King,"
(*Ancient & Mod.* 381)

changing the word "aye" into "still"—

"For His mercies aye endure,
Ever faithful, ever sure."

Milton's grand 'Hymn on the Nativity' was composed when he was a Bachelor of Arts at Cambridge; and, as we learn from himself, it was begun on the morning of Christmas Day, 1629[1]:—

"It was the winter wild,
While the heaven-born Child,
All meanly wrapt in the rude manger lies."

Hallam, the historian, calls it "perhaps the finest ode in the English language[2]."

During this stormy period of English history, there

---

[1] In the sixth of his *Latin Elegiacs*, addressed to Charles Diodati; there are translations of these in Cowper's *Poems*.

[2] *Literary History*, Part iii. chap. 5.

came to the front a name by far the greatest in the roll of Nonconformist Divines, Richard Baxter. The important part which he played in the Conferences at the last revision of our Prayer Book brings him into still further connection with our subject. Baxter was born at a small village, Rowton, in Shropshire in 1615. He early shewed a serious disposition. He was anxious to go to one of the Universities, but got only a desultory education from private tutors, and from his own intense love for books. He obtained a post at the court of Charles I. This was no place for such a man. He soon returned to his studies. At the age of twenty-three, he was ordained and became master of the Grammar School at Dudley, and later curate at Kidderminster. Here his influence on men and his power of preaching brought him into public notice. Meanwhile, the Civil War broke out. Baxter occupied a curious position. He was deeply attached to the Monarchy. His religious feelings threw him into sympathy with the Parliamentarians. He gradually drifted to the side of the latter. He became chaplain to one of the regiments in Cromwell's army. It was during an illness at this time, that he wrote his famous work, *The Saints' Everlasting Rest*. This was the first-fruits of his wonderfully prolific pen. Its success encouraged him "to be guilty," as he said, "of all those writings which afterwards followed." These were in number above one hundred and sixty, large and small. "Read any of them," said Dr Johnson in his downright way, "they are all good[1]." Among them, were two books of poetry, and of course a metrical version of the Psalms. His *Poetical Fragments* were published late in his life, in 1681. Almost every hymn book contains one of his hymns—

"Lord (original, "Now"), it belongs not to my care
Whether I die or live."
(*Church Hymns* 421; *Hymnal Comp.* 473)

It is part of a poem called 'The Covenant and Confidence of Faith,' and is evidently written by one in trouble[2].

We learn, that the late Professor Clerk Maxwell of Cambridge frequently quoted this hymn during his last illness. Few philosophers equalled him in reasoning power or have gone so far in the more mysterious paths of Natural Science. On his lips, there is an added force in the words—

"My knowledge of that life is small;
The eye of faith is dim;
But it's enough that Christ knows all,
And I shall be with Him."

---

[1] Boswell's *Life of Johnson* (ed. Croker), p. 733.
[2] The poem begins—
"My whole, though broken, heart, O Lord,
From henceforth shall be Thine."

Another hymn of Baxter's, a beautiful 'Psalm of praise,' is often sung—

> "Ye holy angels bright,
> Who wait at God's right hand."
> (*Church Hymns* 560)

A word or two more on this remarkable man. At the Restoration, Baxter was made a chaplain to the King, and was offered the bishopric of Hereford. This he refused. In fact, he was now the practical leader of the Presbyterian party. They clamoured for a startling reformation of the Prayer-Book. A Conference of the two parties was held at the Savoy, in April 1661. It shews the unbounded confidence which his party had in him, and which he had in himself, that Baxter produced "The Reformed Liturgy," as he styled it, of his own, to supplant the Prayer-Book. It was the outcome of fourteen days' labour. "I came among them no more," he says, "till I had finished my task, which was in a fortnight's time." This was to be a substitute for the Prayer-Book, the work and the heritage of centuries. We must allow he was a bold man.

The result of that Conference was our Prayer-Book as we now have it. Our present "Act of Uniformity" was passed. The penalties and the execution of the Act were outrageous and severe. The reaction had come. The other party was now in power. Baxter suffered much and oft. Once he came under the notorious Judge Jeffreys, and was cast into prison. But he lived to see the milder and better day that dawned with the quiet Revolution of 1688. In December 1691, "his many sinful days ended," he went, as he himself wrote—

"To join with the triumphant saints,
That sing Jehovah's praise[1]."

It will be well at this point to speak of the New Version of the Psalms, which was at length published, after many efforts by many persons. The dissatisfaction which was felt with the Old Version led even James I. personally[2], and the Parliament in the time of the Rebellion, to take up the work. But the Long Parliament could not decide between the merits of the rival translations of William Barton and Francis Rouse, the latter a member of the House of Commons[3].

---

[1] Compare *Life and Times of Richard Baxter*, by Rev. William Orme. The "Reformed Liturgy" is given in full at the end of Vol. I. of Calamy's *Life of Baxter*, 1713.

[2] This translation made, part by James I. and part by Sir William Alexander, afterwards Earl of Stirling, was printed by order of Charles I. in 1631, and "recommended for use in all the Churches;" but it seems to have gone no further.

[3] The House of Commons favoured the translation of Rouse, the House of Lords that of Barton. The Westminster Assembly gave their approval to the former; and it was published in 1646 and recommended to the General Assembly of the Kirk in Scotland. For the Psalter produced in Scotland on this basis, see page 127.

The New Version.

Hence nothing was done at that time in England. By an Order in Council in 1696, the New Version was allowed and permitted to be used in Churches and Chapels, and so came to be annexed to our Prayer Books[1]. It was the work of two men, Nahum Tate and Nicholas Brady, both Irish by birth, both somewhat impecunious, and both but feeble poets. In 1703, they added a Supplement, containing certain hymns and metrical versions accompanied by tunes, under a similar sanction. These were altered from time to time, without any sanction.

Tate, a literary man, removed to London from Ireland; and, through interest, got made Poet Laureate. He wrote a good deal, especially for the stage; and among other things, *Panacea, a Poem on Tea.* He was not a satisfactory character, latterly improvident and intemperate, and dying at last in 1715 in a privileged part of Southwark, where his creditors could not arrest him. It is a sad page in the history of hymnologists. Let us turn it over.

Brady, chiefly educated at Westminster and Oxford, became a prebend of the Cathedral at Cork. A strong supporter of William III. and the new dynasty, he came to London, and was made chaplain to the King. Often

---

[1] In 1695, there had been published, "*An Essay of a New Version of the Psalms of David, consisting of the first Twenty,* by N. Brady and N. Tate." 8vo.

in debt, he took to keeping a school at Richmond, and died in 1726. His literary reputation rests upon the part he had in the New Version of the Psalms, whatever that part may have been.

This Version had little poetic beauty. It was simple and correct. It was, by authority, "allowed to be used," and now it is allowed to die. But portions of it will always live in our hymn books. Among these, will probably be the Christmas hymn, written by Tate, the best hymn in the Supplement—

"While shepherds watched their flocks by night,
All seated on the ground."
(Ancient & Mod. 62; Church Hymns 86; Hymnal Comp. 73)

and such psalms as—

Ps. xxxiv. "Through all the changing scenes of life."
(Ancient & Mod. 290; Church Hymns 530; Hymnal Comp. 503)

Ps. li. "Have mercy, Lord, on me,
As Thou wert ever kind."
(Ancient & Mod. 249)

Ps. lxvii. "To bless Thy chosen race,
In mercy, Lord, incline."
(Hymnal Comp. 98)

Ps. lxxxiv. "O God of hosts, the mighty Lord."
(Ancient & Mod. 237; Church Hymns 443)

Ps. cxlviii. "Ye boundless realms of joy."
(Hymnal Comp. 519)

and—

Ps. xlii. "As pants the hart for cooling streams."
(*Ancient & Mod.* 238; *Church Hymns* 334; *Hymnal Comp.* 126)

especially as long as it is wedded to the music of Spohr's lovely anthem[1].

Two more hymn poets of this period cannot be passed by; but as I wish to reserve Bishop Ken to the last, we must somewhat invert their chronological order, and speak first of Joseph Addison. Addison is best known to us as the master of English prose. It was for his poetry that he was distinguished among his contemporaries; and to poetry he owed much of the promotion which he obtained. His father was a clergyman, who went up from Westmorland a poor scholar to Queen's College, Oxford, and became Dean of Lichfield. The son, born in 1672 at Milston in Wiltshire, also went to Queen's College, and migrated to Magdalen College. There he resided ten years; and

---

[1] To these may be added—

Ps. xciii. "With glory clad, with strength arrayed."
(*Church Hymns* 559)

Ps. xcv. "O come, loud anthems let us sing."
(*Church Hymns* 465; *Hymnal Comp.* 491)

Ps. c. "With one consent let all the earth."

Ps. cvi. "O render thanks to God above."
(*Hymnal Comp.* 492)

and—

Ps. cxxxix. "Thou, Lord, by strictest search hast known."

there is still "shewn his favourite walk under the elms which fringe the meadow on the banks of the Cherwell[1]." He addressed a poem to Lord Somers on one of the campaigns of William III. This at once brought him into political notice, and got him a pension of £300 a year. He now started for a prolonged tour on the continent. After some stay in Paris, he embarked at Marseilles in December 1700; and while sailing along the coast of Italy, encountered one of the dangerous storms of the Mediterranean. To this storm, we are mainly indebted for the beautiful hymn called the "Traveller's hymn," and published long afterwards in the *Spectator*[2]—

"How are thy servants blest, O Lord,
How sure is their defence."
(*Hymnal Comp.* 531)

"The captain of the ship," says Macaulay, "gave up all for lost, and confessed himself to a Capuchin who happened to be on board. The English heretic, in the mean time, fortified himself against the perils of death with devotions of a very different kind:"—

"Confusion dwelt in ev'ry face,
And fear in ev'ry heart;
When waves on waves, and gulfs in gulfs,
O'ercame the pilot's art.

---

[1] Macaulay, *Essays*, vol. iii. p. 359.
[2] No. 489, Sept. 20, 1712, where ten stanzas are given.

> Yet then from all my griefs, O Lord,
>   Thy mercy set me free,
> Whilst, in the confidence of prayer,
>   My soul took hold on Thee.
>
> For though in dreadful whirls we hung
>   High on the broken wave,
> I knew Thou wert not slow to hear,
>   Nor impotent to save.
>
> The storm was laid, the winds retir'd
>   Obedient to Thy will;
> The sea that roar'd at Thy command,
>   At Thy command was still."

Addison again got promotion by composing a fine poem on the battle of Blenheim, written at the request of the heads of the Government. Other poems on the subject had been hopelessly bad, and had not exalted either the Government or the victory. This we may well believe from three lines, quoted by Macaulay, which can scarcely be called heroic:—

> "Think of two thousand gentlemen at least,
>   And each man mounted on a capering beast;
>   Into the Danube, they were pushed by shoals."

Besides the hymn above quoted, Addison wrote four other hymns which appeared in some of his exquisite devout papers in the *Spectator*, in 1712. The beautiful paraphrase of his favourite twenty-third Psalm—

> "The Lord my pasture shall prepare,
> And feed me with a shepherd's care."
> *(Hymnal Comp. 331)*

The paper in the *Spectator* is 'On reliance upon God[1].' Then—

> "When all Thy mercies, O my God,
> My rising soul surveys[2]."
> *(Hymnal Comp. 497)*

There is one which does not generally appear in hymn-books and is inferior to the others—

> "When, rising from the bed of death,
> O'erwhelmed with guilt and fear[3]."

and one which Lord Selborne places "among the best hymns in the English language"—

> "The spacious firmament on high,
> With all the blue ethereal sky."
> *(Hymnal Comp. 496)*

It is a rendering of the nineteenth Psalm, and occurs in a paper in the *Spectator* 'On the means of strengthening faith[4].'

These two last hymns have been claimed for Andrew Marvell, the contemporary and friend of Milton. Though

---

[1] No. 441. The last verse in the *Hymnal Companion* is not Addison's.

[2] Of this hymn there are thirteen stanzas in the *Spectator*, No. 453.

[3] *Spectator*, No. 513.

[4] *Ibid.* No. 465.

revived from time to time, the claim has never for a moment been made good; and their characteristics point unmistakeably to Addison[1].

We all know how Addison rose in the world, married the Countess Dowager of Warwick, and became Secretary of State, an office he had soon to resign from ill-health. Of him, it might emphatically be said, "He was a good man—a man who trusted in God and so was full of gratitude to God." On his death-bed in 1719, he sent for the poet Gay, and asked his forgiveness, for some supposed injury of which Gay knew nothing. He also sent for the dissipated young Earl of Warwick, his stepson, hoping to produce some effect on the young man. Lord Warwick said to his dying friend, "I believe and hope you have some commands for me, I shall hold them most sacred." Addison grasped the young man's hand, said softly to him, "See, in what peace a Christian can die," and soon after he passed away.

To this incident, his friend and fellow-worker, Thomas Tickell, referred in the poem addressed to this same Lord Warwick 'On the death of Mr Addison'—

"Then, taught us how to live; and (oh, too high
The price for knowledge) taught us how to die."

---

[1] Marvell died in 1678. The claim was first put forward by Captain Edward Thompson, in the *Life* prefixed to his edition of Marvell's *Works*, 1776.

We turn, before we conclude, from a good layman to a good priest and bishop, Bishop Ken. He was born at Little Berkhampsted in Hertfordshire in 1637, and went to Winchester School—a fact of peculiar interest. The death of his parents, while he was yet a child, left him to the guardianship of his brother-in-law, the well-known and devout Isaak Walton. After passing through Oxford, he was ordained, became a rector in Essex, and was afterwards elected to a fellowship at Winchester. It was for the use of the Winchester scholars, that he wrote, in 1674, his *Manual of Prayers*, a little book still in use, and well worthy to be the companion of any young man. To this *Manual*, he appended some years after, in 1697, his Morning, Midnight and Evening Hymns, which have made their author famous[1]. The Morning and Evening Hymns appear in abridged forms in all hymn-books. The Midnight Hymn beginning—

"My God, now I from sleep awake."

is quite equal to them. It is, comparatively, so seldom seen that it may be well to quote two or three of the stanzas:—

---

[1] Though not printed in the *Manual* at first, the hymns must have been in the hands of the scholars; for in the *Manual* there was this Injunction—"Be sure to sing the Morning and Evening Hymns in your chamber devoutly."

"My soul, when I shake off this dust,
Lord, in Thy arms I will entrust:
O make me Thy peculiar care;
Some mansion for my soul prepare!

Give me a place at Thy saints' feet,
Or some fall'n angel's vacant seat!
I'll strive to sing as loud as they,
Who sit above in brighter day.

. . . . . .
. . . . . .

Shine on me, Lord, new life impart!
Fresh ardours kindle in my heart!
One ray of Thy all-quickening light
Dispels the sloth and clouds of night.

Lord, lest the tempter me surprise,
Watch over Thine own sacrifice!
All loose, all idle thoughts cast out,
And make my very dreams devout!"

The Morning Hymn—

"Awake, my soul, and with the sun
Thy daily stage of duty run."
(*Ancient & Mod.* 3; *Church Hymns* 1; *Hymnal Comp.* 1)

was a great favourite with its author. He used often to sing it in the early morning, accompanying himself with his lute. His Evening Hymn—

"All praise to Thee, my God, this night."
(*Hymnal Comp.* 15)

is frequently written—

"Glory to Thee, my God, this night."
(*Ancient & Mod.* 23; *Church Hymns* 21)

It seems now to have been proved that the former is Bishop Ken's latest correction and improvement[1]. So, he himself changed the words in the Doxology, "ye angelic host" into "ye heavenly host[2]." It has been well said that "there is probably no other verse in the world that is sung so often as that Doxology, itself a masterpiece," beginning—

"Praise God, from whom all blessings flow."

Ken was made chaplain to the King, Charles II., and then Bishop of Bath and Wells in 1684, and he ministered to the dying monarch in his last illness.

---

[1] This alteration of the text has been the subject of much dispute. The three hymns, and the correct text, are given in *The Book of Praise*, Nos. ccxlvi, cclvii, cclxv. These are taken from the edition of 1709, giving Bishop Ken's latest corrections. The earlier versions may be found in Anderdon's *Life of Ken*, and in the edition of the hymns published by Daniel Sedgwick, 1864.

[2] Another change made in the third verse of the Evening Hymn was—

"To die, that this vile body may
Rise glorious at the awful day."

originally written—

"Teach me to die, that so I may
Triumphing rise at the last day."

When James II. came to the throne, Bishop Ken was committed to the Tower, as one of the "seven bishops" who would not publish the Declaration of Indulgence; but they were afterwards triumphantly acquitted. On the accession of William and Mary, he was deprived of his see, as a non-juror, and went into retirement at Longleat in Wiltshire, where he died in 1711. They buried him in the early morning at Frome, in accordance with his own desire—"under the east window of the chancel just at sun-rising." And as the sun rose, his friends involuntarily burst out into the beautiful words of his own Morning Hymn—

"Awake, my soul, and with the sun."

He wrote much, including many hymns, but nothing which could be compared with that matchless Three. "Had he endowed three hospitals," says James Montgomery, "he might have been less a benefactor to posterity[1]."

---

[1] Compare *The Life of Thomas Ken* by a Layman, 2nd edition, 1854. The four volumes of *Poems, Devotional and Didactic*, published in 1721, after his death, contain nothing worthy of the Three Hymns. One hymn, much altered is sometimes sung—
"Behold, the Master passeth by."
(*Church Hymns* 183)

LECTURE III.

THE EIGHTEENTH CENTURY.

LECTURE III.

WITH the 18th century, we meet the full stream of English hymnody. So far there had been in this land but drops from the fountain of Christian poetry. The Protestants of Germany, the Roman Catholics of France and of Italy had enriched and ennobled, with many a hymn, their public and private services of God. Those terrible metrical psalms held their own in England against all comers. They threw a chill over public worship. They bound, as in fetters of iron, those devout minds which would soar in song toward their God. It is remarkable that freedom came, though slowly, from the same quarter whence slavery had proceeded. The Puritan element brought in these metrical psalms. To sing aught beyond the immediate range of Scripture was considered little short of heresy. But it was the Puritan element which laid the foundation of hymn singing in the later English Church. It is to the Nonconformists, and more especially the Independents, Watts and Doddridge, that we owe the first kindling of the flame, the first vigorous effort to supply a great and pressing spiritual need[1].

The name of Isaac Watts has not always been held in the high estimation which it deserves, and especially by those who have been unacquainted with his ability and his writings. This has, no doubt, partly arisen from his name being ever associated with his quaint but most popular *Songs for Children*. Isaac Watts was born at Southampton, in 1674. His father there kept a boarding school, and was a rigid Nonconformist, who had been imprisoned for his religious opinions. The son was a most precocious child, beginning Latin at four years old in the Grammar School of the town. At sixteen, he went to study at an "academy" in London, taught by an Independent minister, Thomas Rowe. His proficiency in classics and logic, even Dr Johnson allows to have been remarkable. In his leisure hours, he made many poetical attempts. As he himself says, "I was a maker of verses from fifteen to fifty." But it was at the age of twenty, when he returned to his father's house at Southampton for two years' private study, that the true poetic fervour came upon him. Watts complained to his father of the compositions

---

[1] It has been pointed out that in a catalogue of 1410 British hymn writers, which was made by Mr D. Sedgwick in 1863, there were as many as 1213 of a later date than 1707; and the difference is far larger now.—*Encyclop. Britan.*

sung in their chapel. "Give us something better, young man," was the reply. His first published hymn was on Revelation v. 9, and, with strange taste, was headed—

'A new Song to the Lamb that was slain.'

Its first verse had these lines—

"Prepare new honours for His Name
And songs before unknown."

And many hymns were written by him at this period. Two of them, well known, have a strong local interest—

"There is a land of pure delight,
Where saints immortal reign."
(Church Hymns 519 ; *Hymnal Comp.* 232)

and—

"When I can read my title clear
To mansions in the skies."
(Hymnal Comp. 276)

Portions of these hymns, especially of the first, are said to have been suggested by the beautiful views in the neighbourhood, across Southampton Water. Beyond the "narrow sea," beyond the "swelling flood" of the river and harbour lie the green fields and woods of the New Forest, as of another land :—

"There everlasting spring abides,
And never withering flowers ;
Death, like a narrow sea, divides
This heavenly land from ours.

> Sweet fields beyond the swelling flood
> Stand dress'd in living green:
> So to the Jews old Canaan stood,
> While Jordan roll'd between."

The figure, here given to death, of "a *narrow* sea," has often been noted, and was apparently imitated by Charles Wesley[1].

In 1696, Watts went to be tutor in the family of Sir John Hartopp, near London. Here he wrote the chief part of a *Treatise on Logic,* published some time after, which in Dr Johnson's day was a text-book at Oxford. On his twenty-fourth birthday, he preached his first sermon, and then became assistant to Dr Chauncy, the minister of the Independent Church in Mark Lane, whom he soon after succeeded. But his health, never strong, a few years later broke down. He went, in 1712, for change of air on a visit to Sir Thomas Abney at Theobalds in Hertfordshire. He went for a week, and he stayed thirty-six years, until his death.

---

[1] See below, p. 148. The reference in the second hymn seems also probable—

> "There shall I bathe my weary soul
> In seas of heavenly rest."

But the first verse contains one of those unfortunate commonplaces which almost ruin some of the best hymns of Watts—

> "I bid farewell to every fear,
> And wipe my weeping eyes."

Isaac Watts.

Sir Thomas Abney had been knighted as Lord Mayor, and was, of course, a staunch dissenter. Long after he was gone, Lady Abney and her family still welcomed their distinguished guest. It was in the summer-house of their garden, that he wrote most of his works. And it was in their presence that he declared himself towards the last, to be "waiting God's leave to die."

Watts obtained the unsolicited honour of a degree as Doctor in Divinity from the Universities of Edinburgh and Aberdeen. He wrote, among other things, a *Treatise on Astronomy*, an *Essay* on Charity Schools, and some theological works, giving no small evidence of his general ability. But the first published of his poetical works was his *Horæ Lyricæ, Lyric Poems sacred to Devotion*, in 1705. Undoubtedly, they are not good. A modern critic says of them—"The sentimentalities of Roman Catholic writers towards our Lord and His Mother are not half so offensive as the courtier-like flatteries Dr Watts offers to the Most High...In him, the thought is true, the form of its utterance false; the feeling lovely, the word, often to a degree, repulsive[1]." And this criticism applies, in many cases, to his *Hymns* published in 1707[2], though they are "immeasurably

---

[1] George Macdonald, *England's Antiphon*, p. 280.
[2] *Hymns and Spiritual Songs;* an enlarged edition was published in 1709.

better." His "*Psalms*[1]," which are really hymns founded on the Psalms, not translations, came out in 1719. There are lines in those hymns which offend against all good taste. Yet there are wonderful jewels in that oft rubbishy mass of some six hundred religious poems. The man who could write them "ought not to have written as he has written." They "will be sung, I fancy," says the same critic, "so long as men praise God together." And indeed, they are wonderful, wonderful in their firm clear English, their noble sentences, in that true ring which touches every Christian heart. Let us note a few more of his hymns with which we are all familiar:—

"Our (not "O") God, our help in ages past,
Our hope for years to come."
(*Ancient & Mod.* 165; *Church Hymns* 446; *Hymnal Comp.* 264)

founded on Psalm xc.

"When I survey the wondrous Cross,
On which the Prince of glory died."
(*Ancient & Mod.* 108; *Church Hymns* 547; *Hymnal Comp.* 167)

perhaps the best of all[2].

"Before Jehovah's awful throne
Ye nations bow, with sacred joy."
(*Hymnal Comp.* 45)

---

[1] *The Psalms of David Imitated.*
[2] In the 4th verse, line 2—
"That were an offering far too small"—
Watts wrote "a present," not "an offering." In *Hymns Ancient and Modern*, the last verse is added by the Compilers.

founded on Psalm c. This, the second verse of his hymn, as written by Watts commenced thus—

> "Nations attend before His throne
> With solemn fear, with sacred joy."

It was altered by one of the Wesleys[1]. The last verse is a very fine one—

> "Wide as the world is Thy command,
> Vast as eternity thy love;
> Firm as a rock Thy truth must stand,
> When rolling years shall cease to move."

Then we have—

> "I'll praise my Maker, while I've breath;
> And when my voice is lost in death,
> Praise shall employ my nobler powers."
>
> (*Hymnal Comp.* 495)

These lines have a peculiar interest as having been sung by John Wesley on the day before he died, and murmured by him among his last words[2].

---

[1] It appears in the edition of the Wesleys' *Collection of Psalms and Hymns* published in 1741. The first and fourth verses of Watts's hymn were omitted. The first was—

> " Sing to the Lord with cheerful voice,
> Let every land His Name adore.
> The British isles shall send the noise
> Across the ocean to the shore."

[2] Tyerman, *Life and Times of John Wesley*.

> "Jesus shall reign where'er the sun
> Does his successive journeys run."
> *(Ancient & Mod. 220; Church Hymns 407; Hymnal Comp. 106)*

founded on Psalm lxxii.

The grand song of praise—

> "Come, let us join our cheerful songs
> With angels round the throne."
> *(Ancient & Mod. 299; Church Hymns 348; Hymnal Comp. 498)*

and—

> "From all that dwell below the skies
> Let the Creator's praise arise."
> *(Church Hymns 366½; Hymnal Comp. 493)*

so well known with the music of Walmisley's anthem. Many another might be quoted which, with faults here and there, are simply admirable[1].

---

[1] Among those more often sung may be noted—

> "Come Holy Spirit, heavenly Dove."
> *(Hymnal Comp. 247)*

> "Give me the wings of faith to rise."
> *(Hymnal Comp. 357)*

> "How beauteous are their feet."
> *(Hymnal Comp. 97)*

> "Join all the glorious names."
> *(Hymnal Comp. 518)*

> "Joy to the world! The Lord is come."
> *(Hymnal Comp. 55)*

> "Lord of the worlds above."
> *(Church Hymns 423; Hymnal Comp. 204)*

> "My God, the spring of all my joys."
> *(Hymnal Comp. 294)*

["Not all

Dr Watts was fond of children, though he never married. It was for the little family of the Abneys, and out of gratitude to their parents, that he wrote his "*Divine Songs,*" and his other books for children[1]. The popularity of these children's hymns was enormous. Certainly, some verses would seem calculated to drive sleep and happiness away from every child who heard

"Not all the blood of beasts."
(*Hymnal Comp.* 134)

"O bless the Lord, my soul."
(*Hymnal Comp.* 508)

"Salvation, O the joyful sound."
(*Hymnal Comp.* 500)

"Sweet is the work, my God, my King."
(*Church Hymns* 50; *Hymnal Comp.* 195)

"The heavens declare Thy glory, Lord."
(*Church Hymns* 295)

"This is the day the Lord hath made."
(*Church Hymns* 48; *Hymnal Comp.* 193)

"We give immortal praise."
(*Hymnal Comp.* 516)

and—

"With joy we meditate the grace."
(*Hymnal Comp.* 293)

see also page 129.

It affords some idea of the estimation in which the hymns of Watts have been held, that Lord Selborne in his *Book of Praise* selects more from Watts and Charles Wesley than from any other authors; from the former he gives 43, from the latter 28 hymns.

[1] *Divine Songs attempted in Easy Language for the Use of Children,* was published in 1715.

them. For instance, Song xviii. "*On Scoffing and Calling Names*"—

"When children in their wanton play
    Served old Elisha so,

. . . . . .

God quickly stopped their wicked breath,
    And sent two raging bears,
That tore them limb from limb to death,
    With blood, and groans and tears."

That is not cheerful for children. Still those *Songs* lived. Lines have become very household words:—"Let dogs delight to bark and bite." "How doth the little busy bee." "For Satan finds some mischief still, For idle hands to do." "'Tis the voice of the sluggard, I heard him complain." They may provoke a smile now. They may be very easy to parody. But it is a striking evidence of the power of the man, that even when he "spake as a child" his words seemed to be "graven" on men's minds, as it were "with an iron pen and lead in the rock for ever."

We must not quite pass by a great poet, though not to be called strictly a hymn writer, Alexander Pope—one whose words are more frequent as quotations in men's mouths than the words of any other poet except the great master, Shakespeare. His celebrated ode, 'The Dying Christian to his soul,' which begins—

"Vital spark, of heavenly flame,"

is very fine. But the little history attached to it alone proves that it is unfit for public worship, though found in many hymn-books. Pope wrote a letter to Richard Steele, one of the contributors to the *Spectator*, with two verses upon the famous lines addressed by the heathen Emperor Hadrian to his soul, when on his death-bed, commencing—

Animula vagula, blandula[1].

The letter appears in the *Spectator* for November 10, 1712. Steele asked Pope to make upon the words an ode of two or three stanzas for music. Pope at once sent back, " Vital spark."

Pope's "Universal Prayer"—

"Father of all, in every age,"

is beautiful; and yet it has given rise to much unfair objection, because he applies the title "Jove" to God.

---

[1] The following are the lines with the *Spectator's* free translation :—
"Animula vagula, blandula,
Hospes comesque corporis,
Quæ nunc abibis in loca?
Pallidula, rigida, nudula,
Nec, ut soles, dabis jocos."

"Alas, my soul! thou pleasing companion of this body, thou fleeting thing that art now deserting it, whither art thou flying? To what unknown region? Thou art all trembling, fearful and pensive. Now what is become of thy former wit and humour? Thou shalt jest and be gay no more." No. 532.

The word is really used as a Name of the Unknown God in the mouth of the "savage"—

> "Father of all! in every age,
> In every clime adored,
> By saint, by savage, and by sage,
> Jehovah, Jove, or Lord."

This verse is also well worth quoting—

> "Teach me to feel another's woe,
> To hide the fault I see;
> That mercy I to others shew,
> That mercy shew to me."

We now turn naturally to another of the fathers of English hymn-writers, another Independent minister, the friend of Watts—Philip Doddridge. He was born in London in 1702, his father a tradesman, his mother a daughter of one of the Bohemian, or Moravian, clergy. He was regularly brought up for the dissenting ministry, and became for some years a minister in Leicestershire. At the age of twenty-seven, under the strong advice of Watts and others, he opened what was called an "academy" at Market Harborough for the training of young men. Shortly after, he removed it to Northampton, where he had a great success both as a teacher and as a preacher. There he remained for the rest of his life. He died just after his arrival at Lisbon, whither he had gone for his health, at the early age of forty-nine. Two books, among others, were written by him, of which little is known now beyond the names, but which had a very wide influence during the last century, and not in England alone—his *Family Expositor of the New Testament* and *The Rise and Progress of Religion in the Soul*.

"He was the author," according to Dr Johnson[1], "of one of the finest epigrams in the English language." It was upon his family motto, *Dum vivimus vivamus;* not a very Christian motto, but one which he thus paraphrased—

"Live while you live, the *Epicure* would say,
And seize the pleasure of the present day.
Live while you live, the sacred Preacher cries,
And give to God each moment as it flies.
Lord, in my view let both united be;
I live in pleasure when I live in Thee."

The pursuits of his life gave a strong colouring to the hymns of Doddridge. Many of them were written to be given out and sung at the close of his sermons. They were not published until 1755, after his death. They appeared under the title, *Hymns founded on Various Texts in the Holy Scriptures*, and were in the order of the texts. Other hymns are found scattered through his prose works. Out of the 364 which he

---

[1] Boswell's *Life of Johnson* (ed. Croker), p. 357.

wrote, some are of the highest excellence; and some we should hardly expect under his name. The grand Advent hymns—

> "Hark the glad sound, the Saviour comes,
> The Saviour promised long."
> *(Ancient & Mod.* 53; *Church Hymns* 68; *Hymnal Comp.* 54)

and—

> "Ye servants of the Lord,
> Each in his office wait."
> *(Ancient & Mod.* 268; *Church Hymns* 562; *Hymnal Comp.* 57)

The Sacramental hymn—

> "My God, and is Thy table spread,
> And doth Thy cup with love o'erflow?"
> *(Ancient & Mod.* 317; *Church Hymns* 212; *Hymnal Comp.* 375)

This hymn was added, about the year 1791, to the Supplement of the New Version at the end of the Prayer Book[1], with some others, by a dissenting University printer; of course without authority, and there it remained. Curiously enough, this hymn has been found too pronounced in doctrine by the compilers of some Church of England Hymnals, and has been discreetly improved.

Then we have—

---

[1] See page 95. Also his Christmas hymn was inserted—
> "High let us swell our tuneful notes."
> *(Church Hymns* 81)

> "To-morrow, Lord, is Thine,
> Lodged in Thy sovereign hand."
> *(Hymnal Comp. 343)*

And, one of his best, slightly altered and improved by John Logan in 1770 to form the second Scotch Paraphrase—

> "O God of Bethel, by whose hand
> Thy people still are fed[1]."
> *(Church Hymns 444; Hymnal Comp. 89)*

---

[1] Doddridge wrote—"O God of Jacob."

To the above may be added the following :—

> "Eternal source of every joy."
> *(Book of Praise, p. 286)*

> "Fountain of good, to own Thy love."
> *(Church Hymns 283; Hymnal Comp. 371)*

altered by Edward Osler, 1836, from one beginning—

> "Jesus, my Lord, how rich Thy grace."

> "Lord, cause Thy face on us to shine."
> *(Hymnal Comp. 42)*

much altered by Thomas Cotterill, 1819.

> "Lord of the Sabbath, hear our vows."

sometimes altered to—

> "Lord of the Sabbath, hear us pray."
> *(Church Hymns 44)*

and—

> "O happy day that fixed my choice."
> *(Hymnal Comp. 449)*

We must speak, though very briefly, of the hymns adopted at this period by two very different bodies, the Roman Catholics of France and the Presbyterians of Scotland. It will be remembered, from our last Lecture[1], that the Roman Church under Pope Urban VIII. put forth a Hymnary with the revised Roman Breviary in 1631. The French Romanists, who have always been very independent, made two revisions after that date of the Paris Breviary, and of its hymns. Most of the fine old hymns were omitted; and a very large number of modern hymns, of course in Latin, were added. Some few of these, it cannot be denied, are very good, and were chiefly the work of two men—Charles Coffin and Jean Baptiste de Santeuil. Jean de Santeuil, called generally Santolius Victorinus, was a Canon of the famous Abbey of St Victor at Paris[2], and died in 1697. Charles Coffin was the distinguished Rector of the University of Paris for nearly forty years, until his death in 1749. To him was entrusted the final revision of the Paris Breviary in 1735. In France, this has now been generally superseded by the Roman Service Books. Translations of some of the hymns from the Paris Breviary have found their way into many of our hymn-books. The following examples are well known—

---

[1] See above page 61.
[2] The Abbey of Adam of St Victor, see page 45.

"The Advent of our King
Our prayers must now employ."
(Ancient & Mod. 48 ; Church Hymns 72, altered)

and—

"On Jordan's banks, the Baptist's cry
Proclaims aloud, the Lord is nigh."
(Ancient & Mod. 50 ; Church Hymns 71)

both by Charles Coffin; translated by John Chandler.

"Disposer Supreme,
And Judge of the earth."
(Ancient & Mod. 431; Church Hymns 356)

by J. B. de Santeuil; translated by Isaac Williams. And—

"Now, my soul, thy voice upraising,
Tell in sweet and mournful strain."
(Ancient & Mod. 103)

the Passion hymn by Claude de Santeuil (Santolius Maglorianus), brother of Jean; translated by Sir Henry Baker[1].

---

[1] The following are also translated by John Chandler from the *Paris Breviary*, though in some cases much altered by the Compilers of *Hymns Ancient and Modern* :—

"As now the sun's declining rays."
(Ancient & Mod. 13; Church Hymns 14)

by Charles Coffin.

"Conquering kings their titles take."
(Ancient & Mod. 175 ; Hymnal Comp. 87)

by an unknown author.

["Creator

In Scotland, everything was done that could be done to discourage hymn writing, in consequence of the fanatical adherence to the National Psalter. Sir Walter Scott might address his country as—

"O Caledonia, stern and wild,
Meet nurse for a poetic child."

"Creator of the world, to Thee."
(*Ancient & Mod.* 83; *Church Hymns* 353)

by Charles Coffin.

"O Christ, Who hast prepared a place."
(*Church Hymns* 146)

by J. de Santeuil.

"O Holy Spirit, Lord of grace."
(*Ancient & Mod.* 208)

by Charles Coffin.

"O Lord, how joyful 'tis to see."
(*Ancient & Mod.* 273; *Church Hymns* 453)

by J. de Santeuil.

"O Saviour, who for man hast trod."
(*Ancient & Mod.* 146)

and—

"Once more the solemn season calls."
(*Ancient & Mod.* 84)

both by Charles Coffin.

"The heavenly Child in stature grows."
(*Ancient & Mod.* 78)

by J. de Santeuil. And—

"What star is this, with beams so bright?"
(*Ancient & Mod.* 77)

by Charles Coffin.

"Captains of the saintly band."
(*Ancient & Mod.* 432)

by J. de Santeuil is translated by Sir Henry Baker.

but even he dissuaded them from any attempt to alter their Psalter. In 1564, two years after the publication of Sternhold and Hopkins' Version, the General Assembly of the Kirk ordered the use of the Psalms in metre. This was, in the main, that Old Version, with certain additions. The next century, at the Revolution, the Long Parliament recommended for the consideration of the General Assembly at Edinburgh the Psalter which had been compiled by one of the members of the House of Commons, Francis Rouse, as well as the Scotch Psalter then in use. A Committee of the Kirk Assembly produced, in 1649, on this basis, the "*Paraphrase of the Psalms*," which was ordered to be used throughout Scotland. This was adopted on May 1st 1650, and there it is now[1].

These *Psalms* became household words very dear to the hearts of the Scotch people. Many a time have the hills and glens of Scotland echoed the quaint stirring lines as they were sung with peculiar force by the hunted Covenanters. Sir Walter Scott has drawn a fine picture in *Old Mortality* of the skirmish of Drumclog. He describes the Covenanters awaiting the

---

[1] The decree of the Commission of the General Assembly for Public Affairs is very stringent "......discharging the old Paraphrase and any other than this new Paraphrase to be made use of in any congregation or family after the first day of May in the year 1650."

King's troops, and, in answer to the drums and trumpets of the enemy, uniting their voices "in solemn modulation," as they sent forth the seventy-sixth Psalm—

> "In Judah's land God is well known,
>   His Name's in Israel great;
> In Salem is His tabernacle,
>   In Zion is His seat.
>
> There arrows of the bow He brake,
>   The shield, the sword, the war.
> More glorious thou than hills of prey,
>   More excellent art far."

In the middle of the 18th century, in 1745, some "Paraphrases" of other portions of the Bible were admitted, by a Committee of the General Assembly, into the Scotch Psalter. These were, in truth, hymns, for the most part severely simple in character and rigidly adhering to the words of Scripture. They were revised, and in 1781 received the authority of the General Assembly of the Church of Scotland. But, whether it be from Paris or Edinburgh, we do not hesitate to draw thence our hymns, let them only be good, and Christian, and true. Such, it will be allowed, are these three—

> "Where high the heavenly temple stands,
> The house of God, not made with hands."
>
> *(Ancient & Mod. 201; Church Hymns 552; Hymnal Comp. 223)*

the 58th Paraphrase, an Ascension hymn, by Michael Bruce,

> "Come, let us to the Lord our God
> With contrite hearts return."
> *(Hymnal Comp. 125)*

the 30th Paraphrase by John Morrison; and—

> "How bright these glorious spirits shine,
> Whence all their white array?"
> *(Ancient & Mod. 438; Church Hymns 384; Hymnal Comp. 359)*

the 66th Paraphrase, founded by William Cameron, upon two hymns by Watts[1]. John Morrison and William Cameron were Scotch ministers, members of the Committee for the revision of the *Translations and*

---

[1] The two hymns are Numbers 40 and 41, Book I. of his *Hymns and Spiritual Songs*, beginning respectively—

> "What happy men or angels these."

and—

> "These glorious minds how bright they shine."

Among these Scotch Paraphrases introduced into the revised edition in 1781 should also be noted—

> "Behold the mountain of the Lord."
> *(Hymnal Comp. 102)*

(the 18th Paraphrase) by Michael Bruce; and—

> "The people that in darkness sat."
> *(Ancient & Mod. 80)*

by John Morrison, but altered; his hymn (the 19th Paraphrase) begins—

> "The race that long in darkness pined."

Paraphrases. Michael Bruce was the son of a weaver and died in 1767, at the early age of twenty-one[1].

Although there are to be found men in Scotland who look upon even these "Paraphrases" as rather partaking of the nature of heresy, yet in many Presbyterian Churches excellent Hymnals are now in use.

Before passing on to notice the undoubted king of hymn writers, Charles Wesley, and his brother John, it will be well to sketch in an outline of a body who had a powerful influence upon them and upon hymnology—the Moravian Brethren. These Moravians were descendants of the Bohemian Brethren—the followers of John Huss in the 15th century, who for so long a time endured persecution by the Austrian Government for the Protestant faith. They dwelt mainly in Bohemia and Moravia. They had their chief settlement at Fulnek in Moravia, whence they obtained their name. Scattered during the terrible Thirty Years' War, in the 17th century, they settled at length, in 1722, at Herrnhut in Saxony, about thirty miles from Dresden. There they established, as it were, a new community. To this place upon his estate, they had been invited by a remarkable man, Count von Zinzendorf, a name once

---

[1] The claim made in 1770 by John Logan one of the Committee to be the author of certain of these hymns, instead of Bruce, has been much discussed, and the result has not been to Logan's credit.

well known in England. Of noble family, a member of the State Council, he had very early taken up strange and strong religious views. He himself said, that as he was passing through the picture gallery at Düsseldorf, he saw a painting of the Saviour crowned with thorns, over which were written the words,—"All this have I done for thee; what doest thou for Me?"; that from this time a change came over him, and that he determined to devote himself to religious work. He conceived the idea of forming a sect. Five years after the Moravians had come to Herrnhut, he joined their growing community, superintended them, and largely assisted them with his wealth. He was then twenty-seven years of age. Ten years afterwards he became one of their bishops[1].

The Moravians, styling themselves also the United Brethren, admitted Protestants from all sides, and soon became an important body. Zinzendorf, having gone abroad to take Holy Orders, was banished, in his absence, from Saxony, on the charge of spreading false doctrine. During the next ten years, he journeyed in America, England and many other countries, planting Moravian settlements and founding missions—the first of those self-denying and successful missionary labours which,

---

[1] Compare Miss Winkworth's *Christian Singers of Germany*, p. 305 seq., and Spangenberg, *Memoirs of Count Zinzendorf*, translated by S. Jackson.

whether amid the ice and snows of Greenland or amid the tropical heats of Africa and the West Indies, have made the name of "Moravian" respected and praised throughout the Christian world. We shall meet Zinzendorf again.

We can scarcely fail to reckon Zinzendorf as a hymn writer, when we know that he composed above 2000 hymns. Translations of three may be mentioned, as being in our hymn-books:—

> "Christ will gather in His own
> To the place where He is gone."
> *(Ancient & Mod. 400; Church Hymns 244)*

translated by Miss Winkworth[1].

> "Jesu, Thy blood and righteousness
> My beauty are, my glorious dress."
> *(Hymnal Comp. 274)*

translated by John Wesley[2].
And—

> "Jesu, still lead on,
> Till our rest be won."
> *(Hymnal Comp. 17)*

---

[1] Aller Gläubigen Sammelplatz.
[2] Christi Blut und Gerechtigkeit.

The first verse is part of a hymn, very familiar in Germany, by Paul Eber (died 1569), the friend and amanuensis of Melancthon—

> In Christi Wunden schlaf ich ein.

See Bunsen, *Gesangbuch*, No. 384.

translated by Miss Jane Borthwick[1]. This hymn is familiar in almost every religious household in Evangelical Germany.

The Moravians have, indeed, had a remarkable influence on hymn writers and on hymn singing. The hymns of their predecessors, the Bohemian Brethren and followers of Huss, won the admiration of Luther. The hymns of the Moravians formed a large part of their worship. Many of them were marked by a beautiful trust in Christ, and by strong brotherly love. Many of them, it cannot be denied, were open to the most unqualified objection. They were deformed, not only by a too fervent, but by a false imagery. They brought the most Sacred Objects down to the lowest level of physical language, and even to something worse. They may be found in the pages of bygone works. It is best to let them lie there[2].

We have now paved the way for the consideration of the Wesleys. The life of John Wesley and the rise of Methodism are themselves subjects for Lectures. But there are certain events in the history of the brothers,

---

[1] Jesu, geh voran
Auf der Lebensbahn.

See another hymn of Zinzendorf's at page 137. For Miss J. Borthwick's hymns, see Appendix, page 245.

[2] Some notes on the subject may be found in Southey's *Life of Wesley*, Chap. v., and *The Journal of Sacred Literature* for July, 1864.

which bear strongly on our subject. John Benjamin Wesley was born in 1703 at Epworth in Lincolnshire, the parish of which his father, Samuel Wesley, was rector. His mother, of an eminent dissenting family, had, from conscientious reasons, joined the Church of England. His brother Charles was five years his junior. John Wesley went from the Charterhouse School in London to Christchurch, Oxford, and became a fellow of Lincoln College. He was ordained soon after, and went to be curate to his father. Being summoned back to College duties, in about two years, he found at Oxford his brother Charles and a band of young men, who afterwards became notorious; among them James Hervey and George Whitefield. They associated themselves in religious and charitable exercises, and soon got derisive names, such as Bible Bigots, Sacramentarians, and Methodists. The last name was said to be given them from their methodical and steady manner of life; but it was, of old, the title of a body of physicians or philosophers who worked by method or theory[1], and it had before been applied to religious people. John Wesley joined this band, and at once became their guide and director. Here he remained about seven years.

It is not within my province to trace his spiritual growth during that time. In 1735, he and his brother Charles, now ordained, were moved by missionary

---

[1] Compare the references in Trench, *Select Glossary*, p. 132.

zeal to sail for Georgia in North America and preach to the settlers and Indians in that colony, John as a missionary of the Society for the Propagation of the Gospel in Foreign Parts, Charles as secretary to General Oglethorpe, the leader of the expedition. In the vessel that took them out were some thirty Moravian Brethren. "We contracted," says John Wesley, "a strong esteem for them. I translated many of their hymns for the use of our own congregations." No doubt, these men had a great influence upon the spiritual life of the two brothers. The work in Georgia was not a success. There was also an uncomfortable incident about a lady whom his Moravian friends dissuaded John Wesley from marrying; and he left the colony somewhat hurriedly.

He returned to England in 1738, to find that Methodism had made great progress in the south under the enthusiastic preaching of George Whitefield. The month of May witnessed, as he averred, the great change in his spiritual life, influenced not a little by his intercourse with a young Moravian, Peter Bohler. During that year, John Wesley spent some months at the Moravian settlement of Herrnhut; and in Prussia, he formed a strong friendship for Count Zinzendorf, who was still banished from Saxony. On his return, Wesley joined Whitefield, and threw himself heart and soul into the work of preaching and propagating their opinions. He affirmed that he wanted to call men back to "old Church of England principles." Another object, they may truly be said to have had—to break through the indifference which hung like a pall over the religion of England. Parish churches and dissenting chapels were alike soon closed against them. They preached much in the open air. The first Methodist meeting-house was begun to be built in the horse fair at Bristol in 1739. The effect of their energy and zeal was astonishing. To them, even, at this day, Christian England stands not a little indebted.

As in other times of religious earnestness which we have reviewed, hymn-singing became a powerful instrument. The first Wesleyan *Collection of Psalms and Hymns* was published by John Wesley in 1738. In this appeared some of his translations from the German; but Charles was the main contributor. Then volumes by the two brothers of Wesleyan *Hymns and Sacred Poems* followed one another in quick succession. The book which was the foundation of the later Methodist hymn-books was published by the Wesleys in 1780, under the title which is still retained—*A Collection of Hymns for the use of the People called Methodists*. Among John Wesley's translations, may be named—

"Lo, God is here; let us adore,
And own how dreadful is this place."
(Church Hymns 415; *Hymnal Comp.* 210)

a fine translation from Gerhard Tersteegen[1].
And—

"O Thou, to Whose all-searching sight
The darkness shineth as the light."
(Church Hymns 460; Hymnal Comp. 130)

from Zinzendorf[2].

---

[1]   Gott ist gegenwärtig! lasset uns anbeten.
Gerhard Tersteegen, one of the "mystic" German poets, was born in Westphalia, in 1697, and died in 1769, and was therefore contemporary with Wesley.

[2]   Seelenbräutigam, O Du Gottes Lamm.
often said, incorrectly, to be by Tersteegen. Other translations by John Wesley are:—
"Now I have found the ground wherein."
(Hymnal Comp. 269)
Ich habe nun den Grund gefunden.

by J. A. Rothe (died 1758), a friend of Zinzendorf.
"O Lord, within Thy sacred gates."
(Hymnal Comp. 199)

from the Spanish.
"Thee will I love, my strength, my tower."
(Hymnal Comp. 299)
Ich will Dich lieben, meine Stärke.

by Angelus Silesius (see Appendix page 248).
"Thou hidden love of God whose height."
(Hymnal Comp. 314)
Verborgne Gottes Liebe, Du.

by Tersteegen.
And—
"Jesu (or "I thirst") Thou wounded Lamb of God."
(Hymnal Comp. 380)

from four German hymns.
See also the translations referred to at pp. 84, 132.

Of the hymns of Charles Wesley, we shall speak presently. John does not appear to have composed any hymns himself. He prided himself on the singing in the meeting-houses. He made it an essential part of the service, and contrasted the result with the practice of the parish churches. This is what he says of his own people :—"Their solemn addresses to God are not interrupted, either by the formal drawl of a parish clerk, the screaming of boys who bawl out what they neither feel nor understand, or the unseasonable and unmeaning impertinence of a voluntary on the organ." Southey notes here, that Wesley himself declared, he had once found at Church an uncommon blessing, when he least expected it, namely, while the organ was playing a voluntary. Perhaps, others have found the same. But Wesley goes on—"When it is seasonable to sing praise to God, they do it with the spirit and the understanding also; not in the miserable scandalous doggerel of Sternhold and Hopkins, but in psalms and hymns which are both sense and poetry."...They are "sung in well-composed and well-adapted tunes, not by a handful of wild unawakened striplings, but by a whole serious congregation; and these, not lolling at ease, or in the indecent posture of sitting, but all standing before God, and praising him lustily and with a good courage[1]."

---

[1] Southey, *Life of Wesley*, Chap. xxi.

Some good, if somewhat broad, hints may be found here.

It may be interesting to know what was thought of these services of Wesley's by some of the people of his own day. Here are a few lines from an account of a visit to one of the chapels by a man of the world, a witty but not a very satisfactory man, Horace Walpole. —"I have been," he says, "at one opera, Mr Wesley's. They have boys and girls with charming voices, that sing hymns, in parts, to Scotch ballad tunes; but indeed so long, that one would think they were already in eternity, and knew how much time they had before them. The chapel is very neat...Wesley is a lean elderly man, fresh coloured, his hair smoothly combed, but with a *soupçon* of curl at the ends. Wondrous clean, but as evidently an actor as Garrick. He spoke his sermon, but so fast, and with so little accent, that I am sure he has often uttered it, for it was like a lesson. There were parts and eloquence in it; but towards the end, he exalted his voice, and acted very vulgar enthusiasm...Except a few from curiosity, and *some honourable women*, the congregation was very mean[1]."

As we may conclude, John Wesley was a man of strong opinions. He would not brook opposition. Hence, probably, the success of his organization. He

---

[1] *Private Correspondence of Horace Walpole.*

soon differed from the Moravians, who became his bitter enemies. He parted from Zinzendorf, who had come to England, and, as he said, parted "without the least hope of reconciliation." Soon after, he separated from Whitefield, whose Calvinistic doctrines were far too extreme for him. The two fathers of Methodism remained friends. "You and I preach a different Gospel," said Whitefield. Henceforth, there were two distinct parties among the Methodists.

John Wesley's relations with women do not appear to have been fortunate; with his wife, the most unfortunate of all. He married a widow, Mrs Vazeille, in 1751. The marriage was an unhappy one. He was always busy. She thought herself neglected. She ran away several times, and was induced to come back. She tried the experiment once too often, and was not asked to return. "I did not forsake her," he wrote in his journal, "I did not dismiss her. I will not recall her[1]." For many years after this, John Wesley went on ruling and organizing his great system. He travelled and preached incessantly, and yet found time to write much. He died, earnest to the last, on March 2nd, 1791, at the age of eighty-eight[2].

---

[1] "Non eam reliqui—non dimisi—non revocabo." It has been doubted whether after he wrote this, his wife did not, but only for a time, rejoin him.

[2] Compare Southey, *Life of Wesley;* *The Churchman's Life*

Meanwhile, his brother Charles, five years his junior, had led a quieter life, and was a much more domestic character. He continued to preach among the Methodists, especially in London and Bristol, and died three years before his brother. But it is as a hymn writer that the name of Charles Wesley will live, and live for long. It is said that he composed altogether above six thousand hymns. He was writing and publishing them almost to the day of his death. They are of all kinds, and for all occasions. He contributed the great majority of the hymns in the Wesleyan *Collection*, already mentioned. From the year 1741 onwards, he published very many volumes of hymns[1]. Some are of remarkable excellence, and are justly popular with nearly all bodies of Christians. It is said that some were written on cards, as he rode on horseback. At times, he would hasten home, and rush for pen and ink, that he might put down the words which were burning within him. Very familiar to us are the following :—

> "Hark, the herald angels sing
> Glory to the new-born King."
> (*Ancient & Mod.* 60; *Church Hymns* 80; *Hymnal Comp.* 78)

---

of Wesley, by R. Denny Urlin (S. P. C. K.); and, for further details, *Life and Times of Rev. John Wesley*, by Rev. L. Tyerman, 1878.

[1] A curious list is given in Miller, *Singers and Songs of the Church*, p. 185; the first is—*Hymns on God's Everlasting Love*, 1741.

Charles Wesley wrote—

> "Hark, how all the welkin rings
> Glory to the King of Kings."

but this was altered as above by his brother John, or more probably, by Martin Madan, in whose Collection, published in 1760, the alteration is first found[1]. The hymn consisted of five stanzas; portions of the two last are now often combined[2].

> "Jesu, Lover of my soul[3],
> Let me to Thy bosom fly."
> (*Ancient & Mod.* 193; *Church Hymns* 396; *Hymnal Comp.* 140)

This, in the original form, has also five stanzas.

The third stanza, which is usually omitted, runs as follows—

> "Wilt Thou not regard my call?
> Wilt Thou not accept my prayer?
> Lo! I sink, I faint, I fall,
> Lo! on Thee I cast my care.

---

[1] Martin Madan was the first chaplain of the Lock Hospital, the cousin and friend of William Cowper, and died in 1790. He himself wrote no hymns; his Collection is styled, *Psalms and Hymns extracted from various Authors.*

[2] The hymn appeared in 1739. The two last lines of the first verse, often altered, were—

> "Universal nature say,
> Christ, the Lord, is born to-day!"

[3] The expression is probably taken from Wisdom xi. 26: "But Thou sparest all for they are Thine, O Thou Lover of souls."

> Reach me out Thy gracious hand,
> While I of Thy strength receive,
> Hoping against hope I stand,
> Dying, and behold, I live."

Then—

> "O Love divine, how sweet thou art!
> When shall I find my willing heart
> All taken up by thee?"
>
> (*Ancient & Mod.* 195; *Church Hymns* 455; *Hymnal Comp.* 296)

Few *personal* hymns are equal to this[1].

The magnificent Advent hymn—

> "Lo, He comes, with clouds descending,
> Once for favour'd sinners slain."
>
> (*Ancient & Mod.* 51; *Church Hymns* 69; *Hymnal Comp.* 64)

This is often said to be by Martin Madan, because it is found in his Collection of hymns[2]. It is really a cento, or selection, of six verses compiled by Madan from two hymns by Charles Wesley, and one by John Cennick, who for a time was a friend of the Wesleys[3]. Cennick's hymn commenced—

---

[1] Handel composed a tune expressly for this hymn, also for—
   "Rejoice, the Lord is King."

[2] See above page 142.

[3] Cennick was first a preacher under John Wesley, then under Whitefield; he afterwards joined the Moravians. This hymn of his appeared in 1752. He was also the author of—
   " Brethren, let us join to bless."
      (*Hymnal Comp.* 512)

[" Children

> "Lo, He cometh, countless trumpets
> Blow to raise the sleeping dead."

From it are taken the third and fourth verses, which begin respectively—

> "Every island, sea, and mountain."

and—

> "Now Redemption long expected."

The other four verses are from Wesley's two hymns, which were written in 1758[1], when there were "wars

> "Children of the heavenly King."
> (*Church Hymns* 342; *Hymnal Comp.* 340)

and—

> "Not unto us, but Thee, O Lord."
> (*Hymnal Comp.* 211)

as altered by Thomas Cotterill, 1812.

[1] These are Numbers 38 and 39 in his *Hymns of Intercession for all Mankind*, 1758. In the concluding verse, beginning—

> "Yea, Amen! let all adore Thee,"

Charles Wesley wrote—

> "Jah Jehovah,
> Everlasting God come down!"

Madan made the change to—

> "O, come quickly,"

from a line of Cennick's.

The verse often inserted, beginning—

> "Those dear tokens of His Passion,"

was also Wesley's. To avoid confusion, it may be stated that—
in *Ancient and Modern* all the four verses are by C. Wesley;
in *Church Hymns* verse 3 is by Cennick, the rest by C. Wesley;
in *Hymnal Comp.* verse 4 is by Cennick, the rest by C. Wesley.
Compare *The Book of Praise*, No. xc. note.

and rumours of wars" throughout Europe and much trouble in England.

This hymn has also been often ascribed wrongly to Thomas Olivers, he having written a hymn or ode in the same metre and with the same first line to the fourth of its thirty-six stanzas[1]—

> "Lo, He comes, with clouds descending!
> Hark! the trump of God is blown."

The first line of his ode is—

> "Come, immortal King of Glory."

Moreover Olivers composed the tune "Helmsley" to which it is generally sung. It is said that Olivers took the tune from a street song which he accidentally heard[2].

Then we have the Easter hymn—

> "Christ, the Lord, is risen to-day,
> Sons of men and angels say[3]."
> (*Church Hymns* 134; *Hymnal Comp.* 182)

---

[1] That is in the *second* edition, which was much enlarged and altered. These two editions were published by Daniel Sedgwick in 1868. See below, p. 149.

[2] This is quite compatible with the statement, that "Helmsley" is the tune to a once popular song—"Guardian angels now protect me," and afterwards a dance tune in a play called 'The Golden Pippin.' See Grove's *Dictionary of Music and Musicians* and Major Crawford's account in the notes to the *Irish Church Hymnal*.

[3] To be carefully distinguished from the hymn by Miss Leeson, with the same first line (*Ancient and Mod.* 131).

It may be noted here, that the popular Easter hymn in the same metre—

> "Jesus Christ is risen to-day, Hallelujah!
> Our triumphant holy day, Hallelujah!"
> *(Anc. & Mod. 134; Church Hymns 136; Hymnal Comp. 183)*

is by an unknown author. It was appended to the edition of the New Version of the Psalms which was put out in 1796; but it had appeared before in *The Compleat Psalmodist* by John Arnold in 1749. The *Gloria* to it, often appended as a fourth verse, is by Charles Wesley[1].

Then, his other Advent hymn—

> "Thou Judge of quick and dead,
> Before Whose bar severe."
> *(Ancient & Mod. 205; Hymnal Comp. 59)*

The beautiful Morning hymns—

> "Christ, Whose glory fills the skies,
> Christ the true, the only Light."
> *(Ancient & Mod. 7; Church Hymns 4; Hymnal Comp. 6)*

and—

> "Forth in thy Name, O Lord, I go,
> My daily labour to pursue."
> *(Ancient & Mod. 8; Hymnal Comp. 12)*

---

[1] In a slightly different form, the hymn has been found in a *Collection of Divine Songs and Hymns* entitled *Lyra Davidica*, London, 1708, and appears to be a translation of a Latin hymn, probably of the 14th century—

> Surrexit Christus hodie,

which is given in Daniel, *Thesaurus Hymnol.* i. 341.

Also, perhaps, the most touching of all his hymns, said by John Wesley to have been the sweetest his brother ever wrote[1]—

> "Come, let us join our friends above,
> Who have obtained the prize."
> *(Hymnal Comp.* 369)

How admirable are these verses—

> "One family, we dwell in Him,
> One Church, above, beneath;
> Though now divided by the stream,
> The narrow stream of death.
>
> One army of the living God,
> To His command we bow;
> Part of His host hath cross'd the flood,
> And part is crossing now.
>
> . . . . . .

---

[1] The hymn, in some Hymnals, begins with the second stanza—

> "Let saints on earth in concert sing,
> With those whose work is done."
> *(Ancient & Mod.* 221)

altered from—

> "Let all the saints terrestrial sing
> With those to glory gone."

That in *Church Hymns* 515, begins with a verse altered from a verse by Watts—

> "The saints on earth, and those above
> But one communion make."

> Our spirits too shall quickly join,
>   Like theirs with glory crown'd,
> And shout to see our Captain's sign,
>   To hear His trumpet sound."

The figure of "the narrow stream" is perhaps due to the line of Watts, already mentioned—

> "Death, like a narrow sea divides."

And there is many another hymn which want of space alone forbids us to quote[1].

---

[1] The following are so well known that they must be added:—

"Blow ye the trumpet, blow."
(*Hymnal Comp.* 181)

"Come, Thou long-expected Jesus."
(*Hymnal Comp.* 96)

"Gentle Jesu, meek and mild."
(*Hymnal Comp.* 406)

"Hail the day that sees Him rise."
(*Ancient & Mod.* 147; *Church Hymns* 143; *Hymnal Comp.* 217)

"Head of the Church triumphant."
(*Church Hymns* 161; *Hymnal Comp.* 368)

"Jesu, my strength, my hope."
(*Hymnal Comp.* 310)

"Love Divine, all love (original "loves") excelling."
(*Church Hymns* 430; *Hymnal Comp.* 295)

"O for a heart to praise my God."
(*Church Hymns* 466; *Hymnal Comp.* 305)

"O for a thousand tongues to sing."
(*Church Hymns* 467; *Hymnal Comp.* 502)

"O Thou, Who camest from above."
(*Hymnal Comp.* 8)

["Our Lord

Thomas Olivers.

The following are said to be the last lines he composed, written at his dictation, shortly before his death in March 1788:—

"Jesus, my only hope Thou art,
Strength of my failing flesh and heart,
Oh, could I catch a smile from Thee,
And drop into Eternity."

One word must be said about Thomas Olivers. He was born at Tregonan in Montgomeryshire, in 1725. He was, for a time, a shoemaker, and a man, as he himself confesses, of bad life in his early days, but was converted by a sermon of Whitefield's, at Bristol, on

"Our Lord is risen from the dead."
(*Hymnal Comp.* 221)

"Rejoice, the Lord is King."
(*Ancient & Mod.* 202; *Church Hymns* 488; *Hymnal Comp.* 517)

"Shepherd Divine, our wants relieve."
(*Ancient & Mod.* 348)

"Sinners, turn; why will ye die?"
(*Church Hymns* 500; *Hymnal Comp.* 152)

"Soldiers of Christ, arise."
(*Ancient & Mod.* 270; *Church Hymns* 501; *Hymnal Comp.* 319)

"Sons of men, behold from far."
(*Church Hymns* 101; *Hymnal Comp.* 192)

"Ye servants of God, your Master proclaim."
(*Church Hymns* 562; *Hymnal Comp.* 521)

and that noble poem—

"Come, O Thou Traveller unknown."
(*Book of Praise*, ccexlv.)

The hymns of the Wesleys have been edited, in many volumes, by Dr Osborn, under the sanction of the Wesleyan Conference.

the text, "Is not this a firebrand plucked out of the fire?" He joined the Methodists, and became a travelling preacher under John Wesley, working chiefly in Cornwall. He himself says that his longer journeys were done for twenty-five years upon one horse, which carried him a distance of not less than 100,000 miles[1]. Olivers was by nature a musician and a poet, and died in 1799. He produced only two works of any note, two odes which would have been remarkable even in a man of the highest education. To one, reference has already been made. The other, written in 1770, reached a thirtieth edition in 1779. It begins—

"The God of Abraham praise,
Who reigns enthroned above."
(*Church Hymns* 511; *Hymnal Comp.* 526)

Lord Selborne styles it, "an ode of singular power and beauty." It is in twelve stanzas, and is said to have given great encouragement to Henry Martyn when he was leaving bright prospects in his native land to enter upon his work in India. This fact lends additional interest to such stanzas as these:—

"The God of Abraham praise,
At Whose supreme command
From earth I rise, and seek the joys
At His right hand:

---

[1] See Southey, *Life of Wesley*, Chap. xvii.

> I all on earth forsake,
>   Its wisdom, fame, and power,
> And Him my only portion make,
>   My Shield and Tower.
>
> Though nature's strength decay,
>   And earth and hell withstand,
> To Canaan's bounds I urge my way
>   At His command:
> The watery deep I pass
>   With Jesus in my view,
> And through the howling wilderness
>   My way pursue."

We must not fail to mention one whose hymns have been upon the lips of thousands, who yet never heard him mentioned—Augustus Montague Toplady, the author of "Rock of Ages." Toplady was the son of a major in the army, and was born in 1740, at Farnham in Surrey. He was educated at Westminster School and at Trinity College, Dublin, and was always a diligent student of books. He early entertained decided religious views, and wrote several sacred poems. But it was after he was ordained and at his living of Broad Hembury in Devonshire, that most of his hymns were composed. He was practically a Calvinistic Methodist, of a very strange temper and holding strong Calvinistic views. On these points, he had a bitter controversy with John Wesley[1]. His health was ever

---

[1] See Southey, *Life of Wesley*, Chap. xxv.

very weak. Under medical advice, he removed to London in 1775. There he engaged the French Calvinist Church for Sunday and Wednesday evenings, and set up a private chapel. For nearly three years he preached with remarkable success, yet evidently dying by inches; until, in the midst of his labours, he sank into the grave at the early age of thirty-seven.

These circumstances give great force to some of his more noted hymns, the majority of which were published while he was in London[1].

"Rock of Ages, cleft for me,
Let me hide myself in Thee."

(*Ancient & Mod.* 184; *Church Hymns* 490; *Hymnal Comp.* 133)

was published, in 1776, in the *Gospel Magazine*, of which Toplady was for a time the editor. It is there entitled—'A living and dying prayer for the holiest believer in the world.' The words "Rock of Ages" are, no doubt, taken from the marginal rendering in our Bibles of Isaiah xxvi. 4—"In the Lord Jehovah is everlasting strength," or "the Rock of ages[2]." Almost all

---

[1] See the Collection of his hymns, 133 in number, published, together with an account of the author, by Daniel Sedgwick, 1860. Many hymns have been wrongly ascribed to Toplady.

[2] Compare the verse of Charles Wesley's hymn—

"Eternal Beam of Light Divine—"

"Be Thou, O Rock of Ages, nigh.
So shall each murmuring thought be gone:
And grief, and fear, and care shall fly,
As clouds before the midday sun."

editions wisely change the second line of the fourth verse—"When my eye-strings break in death," into "When my eyelids close in death."

This hymn has been considered by many the finest hymn in the English language[1]. I confess, that it does not "find me," as Coleridge put it, so much as some others. It appears to be open to serious literary criticism. And yet, not for a moment would I attempt to detract one iota from the power of a hymn, which has been the source of comfort on so many a sick bed, from that of the Prince Consort of England to that of the humblest believer in his need.

Three other hymns of Toplady's are well known, especially to those in sorrow or sickness, and possess great power:—

"Your harps, ye trembling saints,
Down from the willows take."
(*Hymnal Comp.* 511)

"When languor and disease invade
This trembling house of clay."
(*Hymnal Comp.* 459)

written late, and, as he says, "in illness."
And—

---

[1] "The most deservedly popular hymn, perhaps the very favourite, very beautiful is it."—Dr Pusey quoted in *Oxford Essays*, 1858.

"Deathless principle arise!
Soar, thou native of the skies[1]."

which he entitled, 'The dying believer to his soul[2].'

Only a little time is left in which to speak of the once famous Olney Hymns. And yet they bring before us the name of one of the best, best in every sense of the word, of the poets of England—William Cowper. With it, we must link that of his friend, John Newton. William Cowper, who had some high legal connections, was born, in 1731, at Great Berkhampstead in Hertfordshire. After leaving Westminster School, he was trained for the bar, and resided for eleven years in the Middle Temple[3]. Unhappily, he had a constitutional tendency to insanity, which, under excitement, took the form of religious delusion. From time to time, the darkness fell upon him. A comfortable office had been found for him—Clerk of the Journals of the House of Lords. Some question as to the right of nomination arose, and he was called to appear publicly at the bar of the House. This, working upon his extreme nervousness, upset his reason. He attempted suicide, and for some eighteen months, until 1765, was under restraint.

---

[1] *The Book of Praise*, No. clvi.

[2] He is also the author of the hymn on the ministry of angels—
"What though my frail eyelids refuse."
(*Hymnal Comp.* 24)

[3] Latterly, he was in the Inner Temple.

We now draw near the point of special interest to us. On his recovery, in order to be within reach of his brother, a Fellow of Corpus College, Cambridge, he went to live at Huntingdon. There he made the acquaintance of a clergyman's family, named Unwin, who were to be his life-long friends and comfort. For two years he lived in their house. The sudden death of Mr Unwin necessitated a change. At the instance of their friend, John Newton, they removed to Olney in Buckinghamshire, of which Newton was the curate. Cowper was now thirty-six years of age. His literary efforts had only been of the most trifling character. He was still haunted at times by the delusion that he was cut off from salvation, that God had turned away His face from him[1].

John Newton was a man of remarkable zeal and vigour, who had taken up rather free Calvinistic views. He held religious meetings at a vacant house in Olney, called the Great House. In these, somewhat excited gatherings, he persuaded Cowper to take a leading part[2]. He himself wrote many hymns to be used at

---

[1] Some idea of his feelings may be gathered from the ghastly poem written by him about the time of his first serious attack—

"Hatred and vengeance,—my eternal portion."

[2] Compare the good *Memoir* by Rev. W. Benham prefixed to the Globe edition of Cowper's *Poems*, also Southey's *Life of Cowper*.

the meetings. He wished to publish a volume of hymns, and got Cowper to assist in its composition. This was the origin of the *Olney Hymns*, published in 1779[1]. Of this Collection, Cowper wrote sixty-eight hymns, Newton two hundred and eighty. Among the best known of Cowper's are :—

> "God of my life, to Thee I call,
> Afflicted at Thy feet I fall."
> *(Ancient & Mod.* 374; *Church Hymns* 258; *Hymnal Comp.* 457)

entitled 'Looking upwards in a storm.'

> "There is a fountain filled with blood,
> Drawn from Emmanuel's veins."
> *(Hymnal Comp.* 275)

The beautiful and cheering hymn of confidence, entitled 'Joy and peace in believing'—

> "Sometimes a light surprises
> The Christian while he sings."
> *(Hymnal Comp.* 525)

And—

> "Hark! my soul, it is the Lord;
> 'Tis thy Saviour, hear His word."
> *(Ancient & Mod.* 260; *Hymnal Comp.* 297)

There are two which tell, in pathetic words, of his own melancholy experience—

---

[1] The volume of *Olney Hymns* was in three Books— I. On Select Texts of Scripture; II. On Occasional Subjects; III. On the Spiritual Life.

> "O for a closer walk with God,
> A calm and heavenly frame."
> (*Hymnal Comp.* 147)

and, the finest of all—

> "God moves in a mysterious way
> His wonders to perform."
> (*Ancient & Mod.* 373; *Church Hymns* 257; *Hymnal Comp.* 278)

This was the last Cowper wrote for the Olney Collection. It was in January, 1773. The shadows were again falling over him thick and fast. The hymn is entitled 'Light shining out of darkness.' It is said, he got possessed with the idea, that it was the will of God he should go to a particular spot on the river, and drown himself. He started in a post-chaise; but the driver missed his way. The cloud lifted for a season from his mind; and on his return home, he wrote this hymn. At all events these lines tell their own story:—

> "Ye fearful saints, fresh courage take;
> The clouds ye so much dread
> Are big with mercy, and shall break
> In blessings on your head.
>
> Judge not the Lord by feeble sense,
> But trust Him for His grace;
> Behind a frowning Providence,
> He hides a smiling face.
>
> His purposes will ripen fast
> Unfolding every hour;
> The bud may have a bitter taste,
> But sweet will be the flower.

> Blind unbelief is sure to err,
> And scan His work in vain;
> God is His own interpreter,
> And He will make it plain[1]."

John Newton, in his early days, had lived a wild strange life. He had been in the navy. He had deserted; had been a slaver, and commanded a slave ship—for years a hardened sinner, and yet a diligent student. When he was twenty-four, he experienced a religious change, and, though in the slave trade, led a new life[2]. At the age of thirty-nine, in 1764, he was ordained. To him, we owe such noble hymns as—

---

[1] Some of the *Olney Hymns* were written by Cowper before this period. Thus—

> "Far from the world, O Lord, I flee."

when, recovering from his first attack of madness, he determined to retire from London into the country. And just previous to this determination—

> "How blessed Thy creature is, O God."

Also—

> "Jesus, where'er Thy people meet,
> There they behold Thy mercy-seat."
> (*Church Hymns* 312; *Hymnal Comp.* 207)

This was written for the opening meeting at the "Great House" at Olney.

Another good hymn is—

> "What various hindrances we meet."
> (*Ancient & Mod.* 246; *Hymnal Comp.* 213)

[2] To his past life Newton seems to refer in his fine hymn—

> "In evil long I took delight,
> Unmoved by shame or fear."
> (*Book of Praise*, No. cccxxxiv.)

See also *Memoirs of Rev. John Newton* by Josiah Bull, 1868.

"How sweet the Name of Jesus sounds
In a believer's ear."
(Ancient & Mod. 176 ; *Church Hymns* 387 ; *Hymnal Comp.* 290)

"Glorious things of Thee are spoken,
Zion, city of our God."
(Church Hymns 368 ; *Hymnal Comp.* 284)

And—

"Approach, my soul, the mercy-seat,
Where Jesus answers prayer[1]."
(Hymnal Comp. 119)

---

[1] In addition, among the best known are—

"As when the weary traveller gains."
(Hymnal Comp. 229)

"Begone unbelief, my Saviour is near."
(Hymnal Comp. 279)

which seems open to serious criticism.

"Come, my soul, thy suit prepare."
(Hymnal Comp. 203)

"Day of judgement, day of wonders."
(Hymnal Comp. 65)

compare page 48.

"Great Shepherd of Thy people, hear."
(Church Hymns 313 ; *Hymnal Comp.* 200)

The original hymn has seven verses and begins—

"O Lord, our languid souls inspire."

It was written, with the one of Cowper's, for the opening meeting at the "Great House."

"Heal us Emmanuel; hear our prayer" (original "here we are").
(Church Hymns 381)

"May the grace of Christ our Saviour."
(Hymnal Comp. 216)

"Now, gracious Lord, Thine arm reveal."
(Church Hymns 92 ; *Hymnal Comp.* 90)

And—

"Why should I fear the darkest hour?"
(Church Hymns 557 ; *Hymnal Comp.* 333)

Newton's great object, he said, was to have hymns which should be clear and simple, and in which poor as well as rich could join. Such he undoubtedly produced, although some are disfigured by exaggerated language. Newton was afterwards the well-known rector of a Church in London, S. Mary's, Woolnoth, and died in 1807, at the age of eighty-two. This, a portion of his epitaph, which he wrote himself, is very characteristic:—

"JOHN NEWTON, clerk, once an infidel and libertine, a servant of slaves in Africa, was, by the rich mercy of our Lord and Saviour Jesus Christ, preserved, restored, pardoned, and appointed to preach the faith he had long laboured to destroy."

We must not conclude without a few parting words, if somewhat sad words, about William Cowper. No doubt, the injudicious religious excitement, fostered by Newton, was most injurious to him. Six years after he reached Olney, he was again insane. Gradually, his recovery came about, aided not a little by the three tame hares whom he has made famous. It was in 1780, when he was nearly fifty years old, that he was urged by Mrs Unwin and other friends to engage in poetry, in order to distract his mind. Then, and not till then, he began those works which have placed him among the first of England's poets. Who has not been gladdened by the purity and beauty of "The Task," or of one of his smaller pieces? Who has not wondered at his translations from Homer? Who has not had to learn by heart—

"I am monarch of all I survey,
 I am lord of the fowl and the brute"?

Who has not laughed at his "History of John Gilpin"? A true poet of nature, who felt that, as he said—

"God made the country, and man made the town."[1]

Four years before his own death, died his devoted friend of thirty years, Mary Unwin, to whom, but for his terrible malady, he would have been married long before. The blow fell heavily upon him. It deepened the growing gloom. The gleams became fewer and fewer, though ever, when they shone, there was the same high trust in God. In the first year of the century, the end came; and William Cowper passed away to "where the weary are at rest," to where there broke over his darkened mind the light of the Eternal Day.

---

[1] *The Task.*—Book I. "The Sofa."

LECTURE IV.

MODERN HYMNOLOGY.

LECTURE IV.

THE 18th century was a dark period in the history of the Church of England. Apathy and indifference characterized too many of Her priests and people. Men of fervent religious views were estranged from Her. In all ages of the Christian Church, as we have seen, the production of hymns has been an invariable evidence of religious earnestness at the time. The hymnody of the 18th century was due, in the main, to Nonconformists or to men who disagreed with much in the Established Church. In the 19th century, this has been changed. With few exceptions, the noblest and the most numerous of the hymns of the last sixty to eighty years have come from the heart of the Church of England. And it cannot be denied, that there has been an astonishing development of religious earnestness, an upheaval of the old sedimentary rocks, a shaking among the dry bones, a breathing upon Her of the Spirit of the living God.

The materials before us are now overwhelming.

Many of our hymn writers have produced, perhaps, only one hymn that has acquired much popularity. It has, therefore, become difficult to avoid presenting what would be little more than a mere catalogue of names.

The first name that we shall consider is that of Thomas Kelly, who lived up to our own time, 1855, although the first edition of his hymns was published in 1804. He was the son of an Irish Judge. After passing through the University of Dublin, he entered at the Temple, in London, with a view of being called to the bar. An earnest study of the Bible and of theological works made him take up very serious religious views. He was ordained in 1792, and preached in Dublin with great success. From this date onward for many years, his hymns were from time to time composed; until at last he had published seven hundred and sixty-five[1]. Among them are—

"We sing the praise of Him Who died,
Of Him Who died upon the Cross."

(Ancient & Mod. 200; Church Hymns 542; Hymnal Comp. 168)

This hymn is, indeed, all but unequalled, simple and yet true poetry. For example, how exquisite are these verses—

---

[1] The last edition of his *Hymns on various Passages of Scripture* was published by him in 1853.

"The cross—it takes our guilt away;
It holds the fainting spirit up;
It cheers with hope the gloomy day,
And sweetens every bitter cup.

It makes the coward spirit brave,
And nerves the feeble arm for fight;
It takes its terror from the grave,
And gilds the bed of death with light."

The Missionary hymn—

"Speed Thy servants, Saviour, speed them;
Thou art Lord of winds and waves."
(*Hymnal Comp.* 111)

and the beautiful Evening hymn—

"Through the day Thy love has spared us,
Now we lay us down to rest[1]."
(*Ancient & Mod.* 25; *Church Hymns* 34; *Hymnal Comp.* 27)

---

[1] These also are often sung :—

"Come, see the place where Jesus lay."
(*Ancient & Mod.* 139)

altered from Kelly's hymn which begins—

"He's gone. See where His body lay."

"From Egypt lately come."
(*Church Hymns* 367; *Hymnal Comp.* 324)

"In Thy Name, O Lord, assembling."
(*Hymnal Comp.* 208)

"On the mountain's top appearing."
(*Hymnal Comp.* 104)

"The Head that once was crowned with thorns."
(*Ancient & Mod.* 301; *Hymnal Comp.* 219)

"We've no abiding city here."
(*Hymnal Comp.* 334)

"Why those fears? Behold, 'tis Jesus."
(*Hymnal Comp.* 328)

Kelly took up such strong opinions against the Church of England in his sermons in Dublin, that the Archbishop had to interfere, and forbid his preaching. He joined no sect, but, being wealthy, he built chapels in several places, and preached there. He lived to the age of eighty-six, a learned, religious and charitable, if somewhat fanatical man.

Few hymn writers have attained the popularity of James Montgomery. Few have produced so many hymns, which, if not of the highest order, are deservedly loved and admired. He had a curious history. His father was a Moravian preacher at Irvine, in Ayrshire; and there Montgomery was born. He was educated at the Moravian School of Fulneck, in Yorkshire, so called after the settlement in Moravia, of which we have already spoken in our last lecture[1]. His parents were sent out as missionaries to the West Indies, and they shortly died. He was designed for a preacher. But he had determined to be a poet, and poetry was utterly forbidden at the school. I say determined, for before he was fourteen, he had written a heroic poem, a thousand lines in length. The following note was placed on the school records—"James Montgomery, notwithstanding repeated admonitions, has not been more attentive; it was resolved to put him to a business, at least for a

---

[1] See above page 130.

time." At the age of sixteen, in 1787, he was placed with a shopkeeper at Mirfield in Yorkshire. During the next four years, he was in various similar positions; but ever leading a secluded life; ever engaged in poetry and music, or in general writing, rather than in business. Even when shopman to a bookseller in London, he could get nothing published. At last a tale in prose found its way into *The Bee,* an Edinburgh periodical. A novel which he wrote, and in which he had too well imitated Smollett and Fielding, was refused, because the characters swore too much. But the boy was becoming a man. When twenty-one, he went to be clerk to Mr Joseph Gales, a Sheffield bookseller and editor of *The Sheffield Reporter,* a paper of very advanced political views. Within two years, Mr Gales fled to America to avoid a warrant of arrest for treason. Montgomery, who had contributed articles, became editor of the same paper under the name of *The Sheffield Iris.* This he edited for thirty-one years. Twice in its early days, he was fined and imprisoned for things which appeared in the paper, things not very serious, but which the Government of the day thought dangerous. A strange training this for a hymn writer. A strange position for one who was naturally mild and retiring, and devoted to poetry. From that time, however, matters went well with him, and he won the esteem of all.

His first large poem, *The Wanderer in Switzerland*

he published in 1807. Many others were written from time to time, the most noted being *The Pelican Island*. It was not until 1822 that he published any of his hymns, although two or three had found their way into Collections. Some appeared first in *Songs of Zion*, others in *The Christian Psalmist*[1]. His book called *Original Hymns for Public, Private and Social Devotion* did not come out until 1853, and it concluded his many poetical works. After he gave up his newspaper, he was much engaged in delivering lectures on literature, and in speaking at religious meetings. His literary efforts were rewarded with a Government pension of £200 a year. He had formally joined the Moravian Church when he was forty-three, and remained closely connected with them until his death at the age of eighty-two[2]. All he said or wrote has to be taken with the reservation, that it is by a man of restricted education, who was a dangerously fluent poet. Still, how much we are indebted to him.

It is hard to surpass his—

"Hail, to the Lord's Anointed,
Great David's greater Son."

(Ancient & Mod. 219; *Church Hymns* 379; *Hymnal Comp.* 113)

---

[1] *Or Hymns Selected and Original*, 1825.
[2] Compare his *Memoirs* by J. Holland and J. Everett, 1856.

founded on Psalm lxxii. It was repeated by him at the end of a speech at a missionary meeting in Liverpool in 1822.

Few hymns are more popular than—

> "For ever with the Lord!
> Amen; so let it be[1]."

(*Ancient & Mod.* 231; *Church Hymns* 363; *Hymnal Comp.* 237)

Of his more solemn hymns, take the Passion hymn—

> "Go to dark Gethsemane,
> Ye that feel the tempter's power."

(*Ancient & Mod.* 110; *Church Hymns* 370; *Hymnal Comp.* 164)

Then the Ordination hymn—

> "Pour out Thy Spirit from on high,
> Lord, Thine assembled servants bless."

(*Ancient & Mod.* 355[2]; *Church Hymns* 253; *Hymnal Comp.* 538)

And how often we sing, without thinking to whom we owe them—

---

[1] Some Hymnals, as *Hymns Ancient and Modern*, omit the last verse (of four lines), which, as the last of the original twenty-two verses, completes the sense of the first verse.

[2] This is altered here, so that the hymn begins—

> "Lord, pour Thy Spirit on high,
> And Thine ordained servants bless."

the third person being used for the first throughout.

> "Songs of praise the Angels sang,
> Heaven with hallelujahs rang[1]."
> *(Ancient & Mod. 297; Church Hymns 503; Hymnal Comp. 513)*

a true Church hymn of praise.

The Christmas hymn—

> "Angels from the realms of glory,
> Wing your flight o'er all the earth."
> *(Church Hymns 76; Hymnal Comp. 80)*;

and a fine hymn—

> "O Spirit of the living God,
> In all Thy plenitude of grace[2]."
> *(Church Hymns 293; Hymnal Comp. 44)*

There is one often sung, still more often with

---

[1] The third line—

> "When Jehovah's work begun,"

is altered in *Hymns Ancient and Modern*, to avoid the error in the word "begun," to—

> "When creation was begun."

[2] The following, found in many Hymnals, are also by Montgomery:

The Sacramental hymn—

> "According to Thy gracious word."
> *(Hymnal Comp. 377)*

> "Come to the morning prayer."
> *(Hymnal Comp. 10)*

> "Hark, the song of Jubilee."
> *(Hymnal Comp. 115)*

> "In the hour of trial,
> Jesu, pray for me."
> *(Church Hymns 391; Hymnal Comp. 143)*

[the second

pleasure read, which is rather an ode to prayer than a hymn, but it is real poetry—

"Prayer is the soul's sincere desire,
Uttered or unexpressed."
(*Hymnal Comp.* 212)

the second line of which is open to serious question.

"Lift up your heads, ye gates of brass."
(*Church Hymns* 291; *Hymnal Comp.* 101)

"Lord God, the Holy Ghost."
(*Hymnal Comp.* 249)

"Lord, teach us how to pray aright."
(*Ancient & Mod.* 247; *Church Hymns* 424; *Hymnal Comp.* 5)

"O God, Thou art my God alone."
(*Church Hymns* 447)

"O where shall rest be found."
(*Hymnal Comp.* 344)

"Palms of glory, raiment bright."
(*Ancient & Mod.* 445; *Hymnal Comp.* 358)

"Praise the Lord through every nation."
(*Hymnal Comp.* 529)

translated from the Dutch of Rhijnvis Feith, 1805.

"Servant of God, well done."
(*Hymnal Comp.* 487)

"Sow in the morn thy seed."
(*Hymnal Comp.* 108)

"Stand up, and bless the Lord."
(*Church Hymns* 504; *Hymnal Comp.* 505)

"To Thy temple I repair."
(*Hymnal Comp.* 201)

And—

"What are these in bright array?"
(*Hymnal Comp.* 361)

This was written for a book on Prayer, which the late Rev. Edward Bickersteth was about to publish in 1818, and written at his request. These familiar verses are well worthy to be cited—

> "Prayer is the burthen of a sigh,
>   The falling of a tear,
> The upward glancing of an eye,
>   When none but God is near.
>   . . . . . .
>   . . . . . .
> Prayer is the Christian's vital breath
>   The Christian's native air;
> His watchword at the gates of death;
>   He enters heaven with prayer.
>   . . . . .
>   . . . . .
> O Thou, by Whom we come to God!
>   The Life, the Truth, the Way!
> The path of prayer Thyself hast trod;
>   Lord, teach us how to pray."

We must pause here for a moment to speak of the alterations made in hymns by the compilers of hymn-books. It has been done, and, I am afraid, it must be done. Authors complain, and very often with justice. John Wesley wrote, as usual, very sarcastically, concerning some who had taken and altered his own and his brother's hymns :—" I desire they would not attempt to mend them; for they really are not able. None of them is able to mend either the sense or the verse. Therefore, I must beg of them one of these two favours; either to let them stand just as they are, to take them for better for worse, or to add the true meaning in the margin or at the bottom of the page, that we may no longer be accountable either for the nonsense or the doggerel of other men[1]." And yet in the Methodist Hymn Book, the Wesleys deliberately altered the hymns of Watts and others.

Montgomery complained bitterly of what he called this *Cross* of hymn writers[2]. Yet he himself altered hymns freely in his *Christian Psalmist;* and there is a charming *naiveté* in the following, when he had been assisting Rev. Thomas Cotterill, Vicar of S. Paul's, Sheffield, to bring out a hymn-book in 1819—" Good Mr Cotterill and I bestowed a great deal of labour and care upon the compilation of that book, clipping, interlining, and remodelling hymns of all sorts, as we

---

[1] *Hymns for the Use of the People called Methodists*, 1780, Preface.

[2] *Original Hymns*, 1853, Preface.—" Yet this is *the Cross*, by which every Author of a hymn, who hopes to be useful in his generation, may expect to be tested, at the pleasure of any Christian brother, however incompetent or little qualified to amend what he may deem amiss."

thought we could correct the sentiment or improve the expression[1]."

In some cases, alterations have been an acknowledged benefit. For example, the change in "Rock of Ages" of the line—

"When my eye-strings break in death,"

already noticed[2]; and the last line of—

"Hail to the Lord's Anointed,"

where

"His changeless Name of Love,"

is a manifest improvement upon—

"His Name to us is Love."

Many hymns, without some alteration or omission, could not have been used in our Church of England Service. Still, this should be done with moderation. In too many cases, hymns have been forced to fit the theology or, perhaps, the want of taste of the compiler, until their sense and living power have all but gone. Sometimes, the hymns have lost their identity, and their parents would not know their own children.

We now approach a band of great hymn poets, of whom the Church of England may well be proud—Mant, Heber, Milman, Grant, Keble. But before we

---

[1] Miller, *Singers and Songs of the Church*, p. 362.
[2] See above, page 153.

reach them, one hymn by each of two writers must be specially mentioned. The first, Joseph Dacre Carlyle, the city of Carlisle may well reckon among her worthies, if it be only that he composed that admirable hymn—

"Lord, when we bend before Thy throne,
And our confessions pour[1]."

(*Ancient & Mod.* 244; *Church Hymns* 429; *Hymnal Comp.* 123)

Carlyle was born in 1758, and went from the Cathedral School to Cambridge, where he gained a fellowship at Queens' College. He at once commenced the study of Oriental literature. He returned to Carlisle, married, and was for sixteen years Vicar of S. Cuthbert's Parish. He was made Professor of Arabic at Cambridge in 1794, and the next year succeeded the great Paley as

---

[1] The hymn was written as "Introductory to Public Worship," and, in the opinion of very old attendants, written for S. Cuthbert's Church when Carlyle was Vicar, from 1785 to 1801. This was prior to its appearance in the hymn book of his successor, Rev. John Fawcett. The two inferior verses on *praise* are usually omitted, and thus the completeness is marred, as well as the reference to Faith, Hope and Love—

"When our responsive tongues essay,
Their grateful hymns to raise,
Grant that our souls may join the lay,
And mount to Thee in praise.

Then on Thy glories while we dwell,
Thy mercies we'll review,
Till Love divine transported tell
Our God's our Father too."

Chancellor of this Diocese. Shortly after, he went out with Lord Elgin, the ambassador at Constantinople, in order that he might examine the manuscripts of the East. On his return home, he was made Vicar of Newcastle, but died in 1804. The hymn, with two others[1], is found in a volume of poems written during his Eastern tour, and published after his death. It was long connected with the name of Lady Flora Hastings, in whose handwriting it was found when she died.

The other writer, the poet Henry Kirke White, fell like a beam of light upon the earth, then passed away. His father was a butcher in Nottingham, and by him Kirke White was destined for that very unpoetical trade. Through the influence of his mother, who was a woman of superior education, he was placed in an attorney's office. His earliest poem was written at thirteen. Besides making great progress in law, he learned Latin and Greek, together with French, Italian and Spanish. He acquired a knowledge of chemistry and astronomy, and contributed prose and verse to various periodicals. At the age of seventeen, he published a volume of poems, which made him known to his future biographer,

---

[1] These are—
"Father of Heaven whose gracious hand."
and—
"Gracious Lord, with mercy beaming."

the poet Southey[1]. He now became intensely anxious to go to Cambridge, and prepare for taking Holy Orders. His wishes were with difficulty accomplished. He entered at St John's College. Never very strong in health, he worked with great energy and under great excitement. Twice in his annual College examination, he was placed the first man in his year. The third year, the tightstrung cord snapped; the frail vessel broke in pieces. Kirke White died one Sunday in October, 1806, at the age of twenty-two. After his death, on the back of one of his mathematical papers, was found that most deservedly popular hymn—

"Much in sorrow, oft in woe,
Onward Christians, onward go."
(*Ancient & Mod.* 291; *Church Hymns* 464; *Hymnal Comp.* 327)

It was in an incomplete form. A few lines were added by Dr Collyer; and, as usually sung, it was completed and published by Frances Fuller-Maitland in 1827. The first line is almost universally altered to—

"Oft in danger, oft in woe."

Kirke White wrote a few other hymns, among them the beautiful Evening hymn—

"O Lord, another day is flown,
And we, a lonely band[2]."

---

[1] See Southey, *Remains of Henry Kirke White*, 1808.
[2] *The Book of Praise*, No. cclviii.

Bishop Mant seems to belong to a day long passed, and yet he only died in 1848. His *Commentary* on the Bible and his edition of the Book of Common Prayer are already old-fashioned; but some of his hymns are as fresh and as popular as ever. Richard Mant was born at Southampton, the native town of Isaac Watts, in 1776. From Winchester School he went to Oxford and became Fellow of Oriel College. After holding various livings he was promoted to the Irish Bishopric of Killaloe, then translated to that of Down and Connor. He was early a poet, and like other poets made a metrical version of the Psalms. He published many works in prose and verse. The most interesting to us is a volume of hymns, in 1837. Many of them were founded on ancient Latin hymns[1]. His translation of the *Stabat Mater Dolorosa*—

"By the Cross, sad vigil keeping,
Stood the Mother, doleful, weeping."

has been already mentioned in our first Lecture[2]. Another, well known, of the same character, is the Good Friday hymn—

"See the destined day arise,
See a willing Sacrifice."
(*Ancient & Mod.* 113; *Hymnal Comp.* 166)

---

[1] *Ancient Hymns from the Roman Breviary, with Original Hymns*, 1837.

[2] See above, page 46.

from the Latin of the Roman Breviary—

Lustra sex qui jam peregit, tempus implens corporis [1].

Also his beautiful Trinity hymn—

"Bright the vision that delighted
Once the sight of Judah's seer.[2]"
(*Ancient & Mod.* 161; *Hymnal Comp.* 34)

Another bishop, Bishop Heber, initiated a new era in our Church hymnody. He not only wrote many hymns which had in them a peculiar beauty, but he wrote many that were well adapted to the Services of the Church. Reginald Heber was born in 1783 at Malpas, in Cheshire, of which place his father was Rector. He went to Oxford, and became a Fellow of All

---

[1] This is part of the Latin hymn—
Pange lingua gloriosi lauream certaminis.
a *Breviary* imitation of the hymn by Venantius Fortunatus—
Pange lingua gloriosi prœlium certaminis.
See above, page 28.

[2] This hymn begins in some Hymnals (*Church Hymns* 491) with the second stanza—
"Round the Lord, in glory seated."
These are also Bishop Mant's :—
"For all Thy Saints, O Lord."
(*Church Hymns* 197; *Hymnal Comp.* 351)
sometimes altered to—
"For Thy dear Saint, O Lord."
(*Ancient & Mod.* 448)
and—
" Son of Man, to Thee I cry."
(*Church Hymns* 502)

Souls. While at Oxford, he gained several University prizes, one of them by his beautiful poem *Palestine*. In that poem occur the lines, in regard to the Temple at Jerusalem, which we see so often quoted—

> "No hammers fell, no ponderous axes rung,
> Like some tall palm, the mystic fabric sprung.
> Majestic silence!"

It is not generally known that these lines are due to the suggestion of Sir Walter Scott. He was breakfasting at Oxford with Heber's brother. The poem was brought out and read. Sir Walter Scott noted the omission of that remarkable circumstance connected with the erection of the Temple, that no tool of iron was heard while it was in building (1 Kings vi. 7). Heber then and there added the lines[1].

At the age of twenty-four, Heber got the family living of Hodnet in Shropshire. Few men have discharged better the duties of a parish priest. He was a good deal engaged in literature. Among other works, he published, in 1812, *Poems and Translations for Weekly Church Service*[2]. This was the germ of his

---

[1] In later editions the lines were altered to the form—

> "No workman steel, no ponderous axes rung,
> Like some tall palm, the noiseless fabric sprung."

[2] Some of his hymns appeared first in *The Christian Observer* 1811 and 1812.

later Hymn-book. One of his most cherished desires was that the hymn singing and hymnody of our Churches might be improved. It is said, that he was only dissuaded by the Bishop of London from seeking license or authority for a general Church Hymn-book. One of his hymns has, perhaps, been more often sung in public than any other hymn—

"From Greenland's icy mountains,
From India's coral strand."
(*Ancient & Mod.* 358; *Church Hymns* 290; *Hymnal Comp.* 112)

The interesting story of its birth is related in Heber's *Life*. He was staying at Wrexham with his father-in-law, Dr Shipley, Dean of S. Asaph, who was also Vicar of Wrexham. On Whitsunday, 1819, the Dean was going to preach on behalf of the Society for the Propagation of the Gospel. On the Saturday before, while some friends were present, he asked Heber to write something for them to sing in the morning. Heber went to a side-table; and shortly the Dean asked him what he had done. He read over three verses. "There that will do very well," said the Dean. "No, no," he replied, "the sense is not complete." And he added the beautiful fourth verse—

"Waft, waft ye winds His story,
And you, ye waters, roll,
Till like a sea of glory
It spreads from pole to pole;

> Till o'er our ransomed nature
> The Lamb for sinners slain,
> Redeemer, King, Creator,
> In bliss returns to reign[1]."

This was but a small sign of the interest in missionary work which led Heber, with certain prospects of high promotion at home, after twice declining the offer, to accept the bishopric of Calcutta in 1823. Calcutta is a vast diocese now. What must it have been at that time, when it included the whole of India, Ceylon, the Mauritius *and* Australia. He entered on his episcopal work with amazing zeal. The *Journal* which he kept during his visitation of that diocese is a most interesting work. Within three years after his arrival in India, he had gone to Trichinopoly. Early in the morning of Monday, April 3, in that hot climate, he had held a confirmation. The Bishop went to have a cold bath before breakfast. His attendant wondered at his long delay. He went in, and saw the lifeless body in the water. A true servant of God had been called away. Amid the universal sorrow which arose in India, many a one thought, in the lines of his own beautiful hymn—

---

[1] The autograph of the hymn was shewn at the Great Exhibition in 1851. The only erasure which had been made was in the change of "savage" to "heathen" in the second verse. *Notes and Queries*, 4th Series, vol. ii. p. 87.

"Thou art gone to the grave; but we will not deplore thee,
Whose God was thy ransom, thy guardian, and guide.
He gave thee, He took thee, and He will restore thee;
And death has no sting, for the Saviour has died."

Heber had intended to put out a collection of hymns, chiefly his own, for general use and as being connected with the Church Service. They were published in 1827, after his death[1]. So many are popular and well known that it is difficult to select. What poetry there is in the noble Trinity hymn—

"Holy, holy, holy, Lord God Almighty!
Early in the morning our song shall rise to Thee."
(Ancient & Mod. 160; Church Hymns 7; Hymnal Comp. 33)

And the Epiphany hymn—

" Brightest and best of the sons of the morning,
Dawn on our darkness, and lend us Thine aid."
(Church Hymns 95; Hymnal Comp. 94)

And the Advent hymn—

"Hosanna, to the living Lord!
Hosanna to the Incarnate Word."
(Ancient & Mod. 241; Church Hymns 383; Hymnal Comp. 190)

Then there is the glorious roll of the Saints' Day triumph song—

"The Son of God goes forth to war,
A kingly crown to gain."
(Ancient & Mod. 439; Church Hymns 201; Hymnal Comp. 352)

---

[1] *Hymns written and adapted to the Weekly Church Service of the Year*, 1827. This contained many by Milman and others.

written for S. Stephen's Day. The first verse only of the sweet Evening hymn—

"God, that madest earth and heaven,
Darkness and light."
(*Ancient & Mod.* 26; *Church Hymns* 22; *Hymnal Comp.* 26)

is by Heber. The second is by Archbishop Whately, added in 1855; it is apparently founded to some extent on one of the numerous antiphons of the ancient Church for the Hour of Compline[1]. Lastly, we have the beautiful paraphrase of "Thy kingdom come," for Advent—

"O Saviour, is Thy promise fled?
Nor longer might Thy grace endure."

which ends thus—

"Come, Jesus, come! and as of yore
The prophet went to clear Thy way,
A harbinger Thy feet before,
A dawning to Thy brighter day;

So now may grace, with heavenly shower,
Our stony hearts for truth prepare;
Sow in our souls the seed of power,
Then come, and reap Thy harvest there[2]."

---

[1] In the Sarum and York *Breviaries*, after the Epiphany—"Save us, O Lord, whilst waking, guard us sleeping, that we may watch with Christ and may repose in peace."

[2] The following are also favourites, written by Heber:—

"Bread of the world, in mercy broken."
(*Church Hymns* 204; *Hymnal Comp.* 387)

["By cool

We have lingered long on this hymn poet. Critics may call some of these hymns too rhetorical; but they have a wonderful charm in them; they cling to the mind; and they are thoroughly congregational.

About this time, during the first quarter of the century, hymn-books began to come into common use in our Churches. We have seen Heber's design. Soon in many little centres, compilations were made, more or less valuable, for local use. It is no exaggeration to say that, since Heber's day, they may be numbered by thousands. It would appear that now, perhaps by the survival of the fittest, three or four good Hymnals are almost driving the others out of the field.

There were, at the University of Cambridge, two

"By cool Siloam's shady rill."
(*Hymnal Comp.* 433)
"I praised the earth in beauty seen."
(*Book of Praise*, ccclxi)

The touching Litany—
"Lord of mercy and of might."
(*Church Hymns* 422; *Hymnal Comp.* 37)
"Spirit of truth, on this Thy day."
(*Hymnal Comp.* 242)
"The Lord of Might from Sinai's brow."
(*Hymnal Comp.* 67)
"The Lord will come, the earth shall quake."
(*Hymnal Comp.* 62)
"Thou art gone to the grave; but we will not deplore thee."
(*Hymnal Comp.* 479)

And—
"When through the torn sail the wild tempest is streaming."

brothers, named Grant, at the same College, and in the same year. They both took distinguished places in the final examinations in 1801[1]. The elder brother, Charles, became Lord Glenelg, Secretary of State for the Colonies. The younger, Robert, was knighted, and went out to India as Governor of Bombay, where he died in 1838. Sir Robert wrote and published several good hymns at different times of his life. A volume of these, entitled *Sacred Poems*, was put out by Lord Glenelg the year after his brother's death. Three of them should certainly be named. The well-known Litany—

"Saviour, when in dust to Thee,
Low we bow the adoring knee."

(*Ancient & Mod.* 251; *Church Hymns* 494; *Hymnal Comp.* 35)

The touching lines—

"When gathering clouds around I view,
And days are dark, and friends are few."

(*Church Hymns* 546; *Hymnal Comp.* 463)

and the bold hymn of praise, founded on the 104th Psalm—

"O worship the King,
All glorious above."

(*Ancient & Mod.* 167; *Church Hymns* 477; *Hymnal Comp.* 520)

---

[1] Curiously enough in the class lists they were together, Robert the younger being third wrangler and Charles being fourth; and again they were together in the classical examination, the elder being now the first Chancellor's medallist, Robert being the second.

Dean Milman's best known hymns appeared in the hymn-book by Bishop Heber, of which we have spoken[1]. Having come now to a hymn writer who only died in 1868, much historical matter would be superfluous. The incidents upon which we shall henceforth dwell will, therefore, be comparatively few. Henry Hart Milman was the son of Sir Francis Milman, physician to George III. He went to Oxford, became Fellow of Brasenose College; and in 1821 Professor of Poetry in that University. The year before, he had published his fine poem, *The Fall of Jerusalem.* Milman was afterwards made Canon of Westminster, and died Dean of S. Paul's. Among his very numerous works, both in poetry and prose, his most valuable Histories of Christianity and History of the Jews hold the first place. The beautiful and, at the same time, scholarly language in which they were written would lead us to expect the same in his hymns. And we are not disappointed. Few hymns are finer than that for Palm Sunday—

"Ride on! ride on in majesty!
Hark! all the tribes Hosanna cry."
(*Ancient & Mod.* 99; *Church Hymns* 114; *Hymnal Comp.* 161)

The third line was written—

"Thine humble beast pursues his road."

---

[1] Milman himself also published a *Selection of Psalms and Hymns* in 1837.

This is almost invariably changed into—

> "O Saviour meek, pursue Thy road[1].

Three others are well worthy of note:—That for the Second Sunday in Lent—

> "O help us, Lord; each hour of need
> Thy heavenly succour give."
> (*Ancient & Mod.* 279; *Church Hymns* 470)

The Burial hymn—

> "Brother, thou art gone before us,
> And thy saintly soul is flown."
> (*Hymnal Comp.* 481)

and the solemn hymn, unequalled of its kind—

> "When our heads are bowed with woe,
> When our bitter tears o'erflow."
> (*Ancient & Mod.* 399; *Church Hymns* 548; *Hymnal Comp.* 36)

This was written for the Sixteenth Sunday after Trinity, the Gospel containing the story of the widow of Nain. This connection explains the refrain—

> "Gracious Son of Mary, hear."

to which so much objection has been taken. Milman, a writer certainly with anything but papistical leanings, only wished to express the bearing on the

---

[1] The alteration, sometimes made, of the fine words in the third verse—

> "The winged squadrons of the sky,"

into 'The angel armies," is very weak.

human nature of our Blessed Lord. Of course, the line is frequently altered; the reference and the sense not unfrequently destroyed[1].

A great and honoured name, honoured not alone in the world of hymns, now meets us—John Keble. A quiet, a very quiet life, and yet a life of vast influence. We must only touch upon it, just where it especially concerns us. Keble was born at Fairford in Gloucestershire in 1792, his father being a clergyman[2]. At the early age of eighteen, he took a distinguished degree at Oxford—a double first—and became a Fellow of Oriel College. He soon entered upon literary work. After a few years' residence at Oxford, being devoted to his aged father, he removed to Fairford, and served some neighbouring curacies. He went in 1825 to be for a short time curate of Hursley in Hampshire; of which place he later became the Vicar. Here and at Fairford, amid the calm unostentatious duties of the country parish priest, Keble lived. Visits there were to Oxford from time to time in discharge of his duties as Professor of Poetry, to which office he was appointed in 1831.

---

[1] Milman's hymn for Good Friday is also very fine—
"Bound upon the accursed tree,
Faint and bleeding, who is He?"
(*Hymnal Comp.* 173)

[2] He was the Vicar of Coln S. Aldwyn, about three miles distant from Fairford.

Of his part in the great religious movement of that day, of the band of illustrious men by whom he was surrounded, such as Newman, Whately, Arnold, Pusey and others—some of whom he may in a sense be said to have inspired—of these I have nothing now to say. Of his prose writings, some, for example his edition of the *Works of Richard Hooker*[1] and his *Life of Bishop Wilson*[2], are of remarkable excellence. But the world has seized upon the *Christian Year*. What hymn-book does not contain "Sun of my soul"? In the *Christian Year*, most of his well-known hymns are found. It has guided the thought and the tone of many of the hymn poets of these later days. It was published in 1827, under strong pressure from his friends[3]. Most of the poems had been written from time to time in previous years. His idea had been, as he said, to go on improving the series all his life, and leave it to come out, if judged useful, only when he should be fairly out of the way. But friends, such as Coleridge and Arnold, to whom

---

[1] This was published in 1836, and is now the standard edition.

[2] *The Life of Thomas Wilson, Bishop of Sodor and Man*, came out in 1863. Keble also edited a portion of his *Works*.

[3] See *Memoir of the Rev. John Keble* by Sir J. T. Coleridge, p. 117 seq., to which I am indebted for many of the above facts, as well as to a friend who was acquainted both with John Keble and his brother. To the same friend, I owe most of the information given below concerning Joseph Anstice.

he had read or given some of his poems, would not allow this. Arnold said—"Nothing equal to them exists in our language;" and he was right. During 1827, Keble wrote many additions to complete the series for the Church's year. He states his object to be "to develope a sober standard of feeling in matters of practical religion," and this by a work in close harmony with the Book of Common Prayer. No doubt, this writing for special days and subjects hampered the flight of his poetic genius. "He was," said Archbishop Whately, "like an eagle in chains." But he struck the key-note of all true religion in the motto which he put on the title page—"In quietness and confidence shall be your strength" (Isaiah xxx. 15). I myself know no body of uninspired poetry, where purity and power, where knowledge of Holy Scripture and knowledge of the human heart, where the love of nature and the love of Christ are so wonderfully combined.

The *Christian Year* was published anonymously, though Keble always owned the work. He had little idea of its importance. He used to speak of it as "that book." Its remarkable acceptance by the whole Christian world, by thousands who differed from him in his religious views, has proved its power over the minds of men. In twenty-five years, 108,000 copies had been issued, in 43 editions. In April 1873, when the copyright expired, 305,500 copies had been sold[1]. Since then the sale has enormously increased, both in England and America. Keble himself lived to make some alterations in the 96th edition, published in 1866, the year of his death. Such a success is quite without a parallel in religious poetry. As we read the book, we are not surprised. "It is a book which leads the soul up to God, not through one, but through all, of the various faculties which He has implanted in it[2]." The poems are not all, from their nature or their metre, adapted for congregational singing. Such as these have now been well proved—

"New every morning is the love,
Our wakening and uprising prove."
(Ancient & Mod. 4; Church Hymns 8; Hymnal Comp. 3)

taken from his Morning hymn of sixteen stanzas, beginning—

"Hues of the rich unfolding morn."

Then—

---

[1] In the nine months immediately following his death, seven editions were issued of 11,000 copies.—*Memoir* by Sir J. T. Coleridge, p. 155. The copyright was offered to Mr Joseph Parker, of the Oxford University Press, for £20, but declined. The selling price of the copies, up to 1873, was £56,000; and there was paid to Mr Keble £14,000.—Notice of John Henry Parker, in *The Bookseller*, 1884.

[2] See Bishop Barry's admirable Lecture on 'The Christian Year' in *Companions for the Devout Life*.

> "There is a book, who runs may read,
> Which heavenly truth imparts."
>
> (*Ancient & Mod.* 168; *Church Hymns* 518; *Hymnal Comp.* 262)

part of the poem for Septuagesima Sunday.

> "When God of old came down from heaven,
> In power and wrath He came."
>
> (*Ancient & Mod.* 154; *Church Hymns* 153; *Hymnal Comp.* 243)

part of the hymn for Whitsunday[1].
And, the most popular of all—

> "Sun of my soul, Thou Saviour dear."
>
> (*Ancient & Mod.* 24; *Church Hymns* 29; *Hymnal Comp.* 16)

In this hymn much of the beauty of the first verse is lost by not having the two preceding stanzas which Keble wrote. The change from the natural to the spiritual world is exquisitely carried out:—

> "'Tis gone, that bright and orbèd blaze,
> Fast fading from our wistful gaze;
> Yon mantling cloud has hid from sight
> The last faint pulse of quivering light.

---

[1] The beautiful little hymn—

> "Blest are the pure in heart,
> For they shall see our God."
>
> (*Ancient & Mod.* 261; *Church Hymns* 339; *Hymnal Comp.* 349)

should be mentioned here. It consists of two verses, the first and third, taken from the poem on the Purification, and two verses added anonymously, as far back as 1836 in Hall's *Mitre Hymn Book*, but altered by the Compilers of *Hymns Ancient and Modern*.

> In darkness and in weariness
> The traveller on his way must press,
> No gleam to watch on tree or tower,
> Whiling away the lonesome hour.
>
> Sun of my soul! Thou Saviour dear,
> It is not night if Thou be near:
> Oh! may no earth-born cloud arise
> To hide Thee from Thy servant's eyes."

In common with so many other poets, Keble tried his hand at a metrical version of the Psalms, which was published in 1839[1]. He only added another to the list of failures. He himself had the wisdom to write, that it was "undertaken with a serious apprehension that the thing attempted is, strictly speaking, impossible."

Ever fond of children, though without any of his own, he published, in 1846, *Lyra Innocentium, Thoughts in verse on Christian Children*, some of which are very beautiful. A few hymns by Keble appeared subsequently in 1857, in the *Salisbury Hymn Book;* such as the lovely Springtide hymn—

> "Lord, in Thy Name Thy servants plead,
> And Thou hast sworn to hear."
>
> (*Ancient & Mod.* 143; *Church Hymns* 141)

and the well-known Marriage hymn—

---

[1] *The Psalter or Psalms of David in English Verse.*

> "The voice that breathed o'er Eden,
> That earliest wedding-day."
> (*Ancient & Mod.* 350; *Church Hymns* 241; *Hymnal Comp.* 454)[1]

Keble died in 1866, at Bournemouth, where he was living for the sake of his wife's health, and he was buried in the churchyard of his own parish of Hursley[2].

---

[1] Keble also contributed some of the poems in *Lyra Apostolica*, under the signature γ. Other hymns of his, often sung, are—

> "A living stream, as crystal clear."
> (*Ancient & Mod.* 213)

altered from one of John Mason's *Spiritual Songs* (1683) beginning—

> "My soul doth magnify the Lord."

Mason's stanzas of the hymn begin—

> "There is a stream which issues forth."
> (*Hymnal Comp.* 474)

> "Hail, gladdening Light."
> (*Ancient & Mod.* 18, *see p.* 11)

> "My Saviour, can it ever be."
> (*Hymnal Comp.* 244)

from the *Christian Year*, 4th Sunday after Easter.

> "O Lord my God, do Thou Thy holy will."
> (*Hymnal Comp.* 281)

from the *Christian Year*, Wednesday before Easter.

> "The year begins with Thee."
> (*Hymnal Comp.* 86)

from the *Christian Year*, on The Circumcision, and—

> "Word Supreme, before creation."
> (*Ancient & Mod.* 67; *Church Hymns* 164)

[2] It may be well to note here that the hymns of Joseph Anstice have often been ascribed to Keble. See Appendix, p. 234.

A year later than John Keble, in 1793, was born a poet, whose Evening hymn has perhaps surpassed even his in popularity—the author of "Abide with me," Henry Francis Lyte. He was a native of Kelso, and was educated at Trinity College, Dublin, where he distinguished himself by writing several prize poems. He was ordained to a curacy in Ireland, and about four years after removed to Lymington in Hampshire, where some of his hymns were written. His health was always weak, yet he devoted himself to his parish duties and to his books. He had often to travel abroad. It was the same story when, in 1823, he went to the living of Lower Brixham in Devonshire, which he held until his death. His well-known hymns are mainly taken from his book, "*Poems chiefly religious*," 1833, and from another entitled, "*The Spirit of the Psalms*," 1834. Among them are many of acknowledged beauty:—

"Far from my heavenly home,
Far from my Father's breast."
(*Ancient & Mod.* 284; *Church Hymns* 358; *Hymnal Comp.* 135)

The hymn for public worship—

"Pleasant are Thy courts above,
In the land of light and love."
(*Ancient & Mod.* 240; *Church Hymns* 483; *Hymnal Comp.* 202)

And—

> "Praise, my soul, the King of heaven,
> To His feet, thy tribute bring."
> *(Ancient & Mod. 298; Church Hymns 484; Hymnal Comp. 522)*

His daughter tells the story of the favourite of all—

> "Abide with me; fast falls the eventide."
> *(Ancient & Mod. 27; Church Hymns 329; Hymnal Comp. 13)*

He returned from abroad to his parish, in 1847, weak and ill. In September, to the surprise of his family, he would preach once more. He was utterly unfit for it. The sermon was a very touching one on the Holy Communion. He was evidently in the last stage of exhaustion. The people listened breathlessly, as to a dying man. In the evening of the same day, he placed in the hand of a near relative that lovely hymn, with a

---

[1] To these must be added—

> "God of mercy, God of grace."
> *(Ancient & Mod. 218; Church Hymns 373)*
>
> "Jesus, I my cross have taken."
> *(Hymnal Comp. 311)*

often wrongly ascribed to Montgomery, as it appeared in *The Christian Psalmist* and elsewhere.

The hymn for the sick—

> "Long did I toil, and knew no earthly rest."
> *(Hymnal Comp. 471)*
>
> "Praise the Lord, His glories show."
> *(Church Hymns 485; Hymnal Comp. 515)*

and—

> "When at Thy footstool, Lord, I bend."
> *(Ancient & Mod. 245)*

tune of his own composing adapted to the words[1]. The second and last verses seem to receive a special force when we know this incident.

Soon afterwards, he was taken south, and died at Nice, where he was buried. The prayer was granted to him which he so beautifully expresses in the last verse of one of his later poems, called "Declining Days"—

"O Thou, whose touch can lend
Life to the dead, Thy quickening grace supply;
And grant me, swan-like, my last breath to spend
In song that may not die[2]."

Perhaps no hymns of these later days have obtained a wider acceptance than the hymns of Charlotte Elliott. For some years she appears to have lived a very quiet and devoted life at Torquay. Many of her hymns were written in an arbour overlooking the beautiful bay. She had much practical sympathy with those who were in sickness or sorrow. Hence, the strong expression of personal religion which characterises most of her hymns. She never married, and died, an aged woman, some few years ago, at Brighton[3]. How many have found comfort in their trouble from the hymn—

---

[1] *Memoir*, by A. M. M. H. p. lii.
[2] *Miscellaneous Poems*, 1868.
[3] In 1871. The particulars about Charlotte Elliott were furnished me by one of her relatives.

"My God and (not 'my') Father, while I stray,
Far from my home, on life's rough way."
(Ancient & Mod. 264; Church Hymns 432; Hymnal Comp. 337)

with the refrain—

"Thy will be done."

It appeared first in the Appendix to *The Invalid's Hymn-book*, 1835[1]. She published *Hours of Sorrow cheered and comforted*, in 1836, and *Poems by C. E.* in 1863. In these books are her well-known hymns—

"Just as I am, without one plea,
But that Thy blood was shed for me."
(Ancient & Mod. 255; Church Hymns 408; Hymnal Comp. 138)

and—a hymn of considerable power and beauty—

"Christian, seek not yet repose;
Hear thy guardian Angel say."
(Ancient & Mod. 269; Church Hymns 345; Hymnal Comp. 321)

with the refrain

"Watch and pray[2]."

---

[1] She was the editor of the later edition (1854) of this book.

[2] These by Charlotte Elliott are also constantly sung:—

"Let me be with Thee where Thou art."
(Church Hymns 412; Hymnal Comp. 227)

"My God, is any hour so sweet."
(Hymnal Comp. 11)

"O Holy Saviour, Friend unseen."
(Hymnal Comp. 326)

[" O Thou

There is one hymn writer to whom we owe much, and who went out from among us, with so many others, now forty years ago—Frederick William Faber. Some of his beautiful hymns are spoiled by a strange sentimentalism; some are good and noble poetry. Faber was born at Calverley in Yorkshire, one of a family distinguished in literature. He took his degree at Oxford in 1836, and very soon established his reputation as a poet. Ten years later, he went over to the Roman Catholic Church. He was well known for many years in London, especially at the Brompton Oratory, until his death in 1863. He also wrote many prose religious works, all of them somewhat mystical but strikingly poetical. The first edition of his *Hymns* was published at Derby, in 1848; and he afterwards added largely to their number. The two which have caught the popular ear are not by any means his best:—

"O Paradise, O Paradise,
Who doth not crave for rest?"
(Ancient & Mod. 234; Church Hymns 473; Hymnal Comp. 475)

and—'The Pilgrims of the Night'—

"Hark, hark, my soul! Angelic songs are swelling."
(Ancient & Mod. 223; Hymnal Comp. 366)

"O Thou, the contrite sinner's Friend."
(Hymnal Comp. 139)

and—

"Thou glorious Sun of righteousness."
(Church Hymns 49)

This last, as Bishop Alexander quaintly puts it, "combines every conceivable violation of every conceivable rule with every conceivable beauty." But whatever its faults, it somehow finds its way to the hearts of Christian people. Another favourite is the lovely Evening hymn—

> "Sweet Saviour, bless us ere we go;
> Thy Word into our minds instil."
> *(Ancient & Mod. 28; Church Hymns 30; Hymnal Comp. 25)*

We will only add that most solemn hymn for Good Friday—

> "O come, and mourn with me a while,
> O come ye to the Saviour's side[1]."
> *(Ancient & Mod. 114; Church Hymns 122; Hymnal Comp. 170)*

---

[1] The refrain of this hymn—

> "Jesus, our Love, is crucified,"

should not, as in some Hymnals, be altered to "Jesus our Lord." It was founded upon the saying of Ignatius in his letter to the Romans on his way to martyrdom—"I am full of desire to die for the sake of Christ. My Love has been crucified"—chap. vii. The same expression occurs at the beginning of one of John Mason's *Spiritual Songs* (1683)—

> "My Lord, my Love was crucified,
> He all the pains did bear."

These by Faber are also familiar—

> "Have mercy on us, God most high."
> *(Ancient & Mod. 162)*
> "Jesus is God: the solid earth."
> *(Ancient & Mod. 170)*

[" My God,

a hymn which, as Bishop Bickersteth well says, "can only be rightly sung when kneeling in thought by the Cross of Jesus."

One name has already been very frequently mentioned in these Lectures, that of John Mason Neale. He has probably had a greater influence on English hymnody than any other man in this century. He was born in London, in 1818, the son of a clergyman, and went to Trinity College, Cambridge. Ten times he gained the Seatonian prize poem, a feat without a parallel. After his ordination, he devoted himself unceasingly to ministerial and literary work. His talents both as a poet and a linguist were remarkable. Besides his general works, his publications on the Eastern Church are of great value. He had unequalled power in translating hymns from other languages, retaining the force and fire of the original, and often the metre in which they were written[1]. We need only

---

"My God, how wonderful Thou art."
(*Ancient & Mod.* 169; *Church Hymns* 433)

and—

"Souls of men, why will ye scatter."
(*Hymnal Comp.* 158)

[1] Most of these are found in *Mediæval Hymns and Sequences* (1st edition, 1851) and *Hymns of the Eastern Church* (1st edition, 1862). The following, as being often sung, may also be noted:—

"By precepts taught of ages past."
(*Ancient & Mod.* 85)

[from the

add two to the many already named. The popular hymn—

from the ancient Lenten hymn—

   Ex more docti mystico.

  "Christ is gone up; yet ere He passed."
   (Ancient & Mod. 352; *Church Hymns* 170)

  "Creator of the starry height."
   (Ancient & Mod. 45; *Church Hymns* 65)

from the *Roman-Breviary* version—

   Creator alme siderum,

of the ancient Latin hymn—

   Conditor alme siderum.

The Harvest hymn—

  "God the Father, Whose creation."
   (Ancient & Mod. 385)

  "Draw nigh, and take the Body of the Lord."
   (Ancient & Mod. 313; *Church Hymns* 207)

(*Hymnal Comp.* 383 begins—"Come, take by faith the Body of your Lord") from a Latin hymn, probably of the 8th century—

   Sancti venite, Christi Corpus sumite.

  "Draw nigh, draw nigh, Emmanuel."
   (Hymnal Comp. 56)

(*Ancient and Mod.* 49 begins—"O come, O come, Emmanuel") from the Latin, probably of the 12th century—

   Veni, veni, Emmanuel.

  "How vain the cruel Herod's fear."
   (Ancient & Mod. 75)

from the Latin of the 5th century—

   Hostis Herodes impie.

  "Light's abode, celestial Salem."
   (Ancient & Mod. 232)

          [from the

"To the Name that brings Salvation
Honour, worship, laud, we pay."
(Ancient & Mod. 179; *Church Hymns* 536; *Hymnal Comp.* 523)

which is a translation from a Latin hymn—

Gloriosi Salvatoris nominis præconia.

of German origin in the 15th century. And a delightful little Evening hymn—

"The day, O Lord, is spent,
Abide with us, and rest."
(Hymnal Comp. 21)

from his *Hymns for Children* (1842). Soon after his marriage, Neale became Warden of Sackville College, East Grinstead, where he remained and laboured for above twenty years, until his death in 1866. No mediæval research, no wandering among the strange

---

from the Latin, probably of the 15th century—

Jerusalem luminosa, veræ pacis visio.

"O Love, how deep, how broad, how high."
(Ancient & Mod. 173; *Church Hymns* 472)

also from the Latin, of the 15th century, beginning—

Apparuit benignitas.

"O sons and daughters, let us sing."
(Ancient & Mod. 130)

from the Latin of the 12th century, but much altered in the above version—

O filii et filiæ.

and—

"O, what the joy and the glory must be."
(Ancient & Mod. 235; *Church Hymns* 476)

ordinances and phantasies of the Eastern Church, ever drew John Mason Neale away from the pure simple faith in his Saviour, Jesus Christ.

Doubtless, when we have concluded, some may well say—" We have heard nothing of such a well-known hymn, or of that great hymn-writer." We ought, as I pointed out, to avoid the risk of a mere list of names or a bare catalogue of hymns. And yet, before we turn to our two last hymn-poets, I will run that risk by simply mentioning six or seven of the best known hymns of this century and their authors.

> "Our blest Redeemer, ere He breathed
> His tender last farewell."
> (*Ancient & Mod.* 207; *Church Hymns* 481; *Hymnal Comp.* 253)

was written by Harriet Auber, who was born in London in 1773. It occurs in her work, *The Spirit of the Psalms*[1], published in 1829.

The Missionary hymn—

> "Thou Whose almighty word
> Chaos and darkness heard."
> (*Ancient & Mod.* 360; *Church Hymns* 528; *Hymnal Comp.* 118)

was written in 1813 by Rev. John Marriott, Rector of Church Lawford in Warwickshire, who died in 1825.

---

[1] Also the hymn—
> "O praise our great and gracious Lord."
> (*Ancient & Mod.* 294)

Miss Auber died in 1862, at Hoddesdon in Hertfordshire.

The well-known Litany hymn—

"Lord, in this Thy mercy's day,
Ere it pass for aye away."
(*Ancient & Mod.* 94; *Church Hymns* 419; *Hymnal Comp.* 488)

is by Rev. Isaac Williams of Oxford, the author of so many beautiful sacred pieces. This is a portion of his long poem, *The Baptistery*[1].

---

[1] *The Baptistery* was published in 1842. Isaac Williams was born in 1802; he became Fellow of Trinity College, Oxford, and afterwards Curate with the Rev. Thomas Keble at Bisley, in Gloucestershire. He died in 1865. Mention has already been made (see page 125) of—

"Disposer Supreme."

He also wrote:—

"Be Thou my Guardian and my Guide."
(*Ancient & Mod.* 282)

"O Holy Ghost, Thou God of peace."
(*Church Hymns* 448)

and the following translations, in his *Hymns from the Parisian Breviary*, 1839, the last two Latin hymns being by C. Coffin—

"O heavenly Jerusalem,
Of everlasting halls."
(*Ancient & Mod.* 429)
Cœlestis O Jerusalem.

"Great Mover of all hearts, Whose hand."
(*Ancient & Mod.* 262)
Supreme Motor cordium.

and—

"Morn of morns and day of days."
(*Ancient & Mod.* 33)
Die dierum principe.

[another

"The roseate hues of early dawn
The brightness of the day."
(*Ancient & Mod.* 229; *Church Hymns* 514; *Hymnal Comp.* 313)

by Cecil Frances Alexander, wife of the Bishop of Derry, and the composer of so many delightful children's hymns[1].

---

another translation of the last Latin hymn, by Rev. J. Ellerton, begins—

"Morn of morns, the best and first."
(*Church Hymns* 36)

[1] Especially in her excellent *Hymns for Little Children*, published in 1848, when she was Miss Humphreys. Very familiar also are these:—

"Jesus calls us, o'er the tumult."
(*Ancient & Mod.* 403; *Church Hymns* 404; *Hymnal Comp.* 318)

This and the hymn in the text first appeared in the Christian Knowledge Society's Hymn Book, 1853.

"When wounded sore the stricken soul."
(*Ancient & Mod.* 183; *Hymnal Comp.* 121)

also the two Passion hymns—

"Forgive them, O my Father."
(*Ancient & Mod.* 115)

"His are the thousand sparkling rills."
(*Ancient & Mod.* 119)

and these for children—

"Once in royal David's city."
(*Ancient & Mod.* 329; *Church Hymns* 576; *Hymnal Comp.* 414)

"There is a green hill far away."
(*Ancient & Mod.* 332; *Church Hymns* 577; *Hymnal Comp.* 420)

"We are but little children weak."
(*Ancient & Mod.* 331; *Church Hymns* 579)

"I heard the voice of Jesus say,
Come unto Me and rest."
(*Ancient & Mod.* 257; *Church Hymns* 388; *Hymnal Comp.* 267)

by Dr Horatius Bonar of the Free Church of Scotland. It is in his first Series of *Hymns of Faith and Hope* under the heading 'The Voice from Galilee[1].'

---

[1] The 1st Series came out in 1857; a 2nd and 3rd Series have since appeared. In them are also the following :—

"A few more years shall roll."
(*Ancient & Mod.* 288; *Church Hymns* 328; *Hymnal Comp.* 82)

"Come, Lord, and tarry not."
(*Church Hymns* 349)

"Go, labour on; spend and be spent."
(*Hymnal Comp.* 109)

the Sacramental hymn—

"Here, O my Lord, I see Thee face to face."
(*Church Hymns* 209; *Hymnal Comp.* 386)

"I lay my sins on Jesus."
(*Hymnal Comp.* 144)

"I was a wandering sheep."
(*Ancient & Mod.* 258; *Hymnal Comp.* 141)

"No; not despairingly."
(*Hymnal Comp.* 136)

"The Church has waited long."
(*Church Hymns* 508; *Hymnal Comp.* 61)

and—

"Thy way, not mine, O Lord."
(*Ancient & Mod.* 265; *Church Hymns* 533; *Hymnal Comp.* 467)

Lastly—
> "Onward, Christian soldiers,
> Marching as to war."
>
> *(Ancient & Mod. 391; Church Hymns 480; Hymnal Comp. 322)*

a hymn, which Arthur Sullivan's spirited tune has done much to make popular. It is by the Rev. Sabine Baring-Gould, and first appeared in 1865[1].

The two hymn-poets, whom I have reserved to the last, are John Henry Newman and Frances Ridley Havergal. Cardinal Newman has made his mark upon his generation. The time has not yet come to form the story of his life. He has himself supplied considerable material in his *Apologia*, which he put out some years ago[2]. He was born in the city of London in 1801, the son of a banker. From his very school-boy days, he was a poet and a musician. In the examinations at Oxford, he did not take the high position expected of him; while his brother Francis was a double first. But

---

[1] To Baring-Gould are also due the Child's Evening hymn—
> "Now the day is over."
>
> *(Ancient & Mod. 346; Church Hymns 24; Hymnal Comp. 412)*
>
> "On the Resurrection morning."
>
> *(Church Hymns 479)*

and—
> "Through the night of doubt and sorrow.'
>
> *(Ancient & Mod. 274; Church Hymns 532; Hymnal Comp. 341)*

from the Danish of Bernhardt Severin Ingemann, born in 1789.

[2] *Apologia pro Vita Sua*, 1864.

in 1823, he was elected a Fellow, and, the year after, a Tutor of Oriel College, and was thrown into that society whose members made such a stir in the religious world. With these and their movement, we have here nothing to do. For years, Newman's influence at Oxford was immense. In 1832, a change was coming over him as well as over the religious world around. Doubt and gloom hung before him. He gave up his college duties, he tells us, and went abroad with his friend, Hurrell Froude. During that expedition, were written the "Verses" which afterwards appeared in *Lyra Apostolica*. They were begun in Rome. The next year, Newman caught a fever while travelling in the interior of Sicily. Dangerously ill, and often despondent, he yet felt, he says, that he should not die. He told his servant—"I have a work to do in England." He was kept a week at Palermo waiting for a vessel. At length, he got off in an orange boat going to Marseilles. They were becalmed a whole week in the Straits of Bonifacio. There it was he wrote the hymn—

"Lead, kindly Light, amid the encircling gloom."
(*Ancient & Mod.* 266; *Church Hymns* 409; *Hymnal Comp.* 18)

with which we are all so familiar. No one can read the lines, and not see how much the writer was affected by the circumstances in which he was placed. "Lead, kindly Light" was first published in the *British Magazine*, and in 1836 in *Lyra Apostolica*, under the heading 'The Pillar of the Cloud,' and with the note "At sea, June 16, 1833[1]."

Another favourite hymn, by Newman, is—

> "Praise to the Holiest in the height,
> And in the depth be praise."
> *(Ancient & Mod.* 172; *Church Hymns* 487)

It occurs in a mystical, but in parts very beautiful, poem, called *The Dream of Gerontius*, published in 1856. It purposes to be the experience of the soul of Gerontius after death. The hymn is a selection from many stanzas, which are sung by five successive choirs of angels or "angelicals[2]."

On his return from Italy, Newman threw himself into the troublous waves of that great religious

---

[1] Also in a Collection entitled *Verses on Various Occasions*, 1868.

[2] Newman is also the author of—

> "Come, Holy Ghost, Who ever One."
> *(Ancient & Mod.* 9; *Church Hymns* 347)

from the Ambrosian Latin hymn for the Third Hour—

> Nunc Sancte, nobis, Spiritus.

and—

> "Now that the daylight dies away."
> *(Ancient & Mod.* 16)

from the Latin hymn—

> Te lucis ante terminum.

referred to at page 22.

movement. Other storms, borne by other winds, have arisen since then. It was not till 1845 that he joined the Roman Catholic Church. It was evident to some that he had been long drifting away. At length the strain became too great. The cables broke, and he went.

The hymns of few writers have come so rapidly and deservedly into use and notice as those of Frances Ridley Havergal. She was born in 1836, at Astley in Worcestershire, of which place her father was the Rector. It was from her father, the well-known author of Havergal's *Psalmody*, that she inherited her remarkable poetical and musical talents. She wrote verses at the early age of seven. Her memory was astonishing. She knew by heart the New Testament, the Psalms, and much of the Old Testament. It is said, that she could play through Handel and much of Beethoven and Mendelssohn, without notes. Her poetical inspiration was singular. At times, she could scarcely produce verses at all. At others, they sprang up, as it were, unbidden and unsought. "I have not had a single poem come to me for some time," she writes in 1868, "till last night, when one shot into my mind. All my best have come in that way." The details of her private life are scarcely adapted to our subject. Her life was the outcome of a singularly beautiful character; a character animated by a great love for those around her and above all for her Divine Master[1]. Some of her expressions, both in prose and verse, might seem too high-flown, too emotional for this plain work-day life; but they have the true Christian tone about them.

Concerning her hymns, we note the somewhat curious fact, that there are more of them in *Hymns Ancient and Modern* than in the two other Hymnals to which we refer. Though they have points of weakness here and there, some of these hymns are very beautiful, and doubtless they will live. Such are the Advent hymn—

> "Thou art coming, O my Saviour,
> Thou art coming, O my King."
> (*Ancient & Mod.* 203; *Hymnal Comp.* 71)

and—

> "Lord, speak to me, that I may speak
> In living echoes of Thy tone."
> (*Ancient & Mod.* 356; *Hymnal Comp.* 316)

also—

> "I could not do without Thee,
> O Saviour of the lost."
> (*Ancient & Mod.* 186; *Hymnal Comp.* 137)

The last verse is worth quoting—

> "I could not do without Thee,
>   For years are fleeting fast,
> And soon in solemn loneness
>   The river must be passed;

---

[1] Compare *Memorials of Frances Ridley Havergal*, by M. V. G. H.

> But Thou wilt never leave me,
>   And though the waves roll high,
> I know Thou wilt be near me,
>   And whisper, 'It is I'.[1]"

I have a little theory about one of her hymns—

> "I gave My Life for thee,
>   My precious blood I shed[2]."
> (*Hymnal Comp.* 304)

It will be remembered[3], that Count von Zinzendorf, the head of the Moravian body, said that he was led to devote himself to God by the sight of a picture in the gallery at Düsseldorf—a picture of our Saviour crowned with thorns and the writing above it, "All this have I done for thee. What doest thou for Me?" In the *Memorials* of Frances Havergal, we are told, that this

---

[1] Besides those in the text, the two following are very popular—

> "O Saviour, precious Saviour,
>   Whom yet unseen we love."
> (*Ancient & Mod.* 307)

> "To Thee, O Comforter Divine."
> (*Ancient & Mod.* 212)

[2] This is altered in some Hymnals to—

> "Thy Life was given for me."
> (*Ancient & Mod.* 259; *Church Hymns* 286)

but the other form was preferred by the author.

[3] See page 131.

hymn first appeared in *Good Words*. It was written in Germany in 1858. She had come in weary, and she sat down opposite a picture with that motto. At once the lines flashed upon her. Now she was at school at Düsseldorf, and afterwards visited the place. It is more than probable that she was inspired by the same picture, or a copy of it, which had moved that other hymn-poet above one hundred years before.

Frances Havergal died, aged forty-two, at Swansea, in 1879. Only a few minutes before her death, while she was, as it were, lying before "the golden gates," she sang clearly though faintly, to a tune which she had herself composed, the first verse of the hymn—

"Jesus, I will trust Thee, trust Thee with my soul;
Guilty, lost, and helpless, Thou can'st make me whole.
There is none in heaven, or on earth, like Thee:
Thou hast died for sinners; therefore, Lord, for me."

(*Hymnal Comp.* 159)[1]

It was as though she would carry out the high resolve of the inspired Psalmist, "I will sing praise to my God while I have my being" (Ps. civ. 33).

Our course of Lectures is over; my long long story is told. The solemn thought of that last line—

"Thou hast died for sinners; therefore, Lord, for me."

---

[1] Written by Mrs M. J. Walker, wife of Rev. Edward Walker, formerly Rector of Cheltenham.

has been in the hearts, and, in other words, on the lips of almost all the great and various hymn-writers of whom we have spoken; Yes, in their hearts, when the time came that kings and bishops, judges and statesmen, ministers of the Word and monks and devoted women, in every age and in every land, had all but one common hope—the hope which is in Him. And it will be seen why I have brought together these two hymn-poets at the last, two so different as the Roman Cardinal and the humble Evangelical Christian lady, so different, and yet one in their love of Christ. They alone would almost suffice for the point I said I would try to prove—that there is, at the bottom, a wondrous unity among Christian men. Glad indeed shall I be if that true Christ-like feeling of unity shall have been traced throughout these Lectures on "Christian hymns and hymn-writers." Of that feeling may be said, what our great poet has said of prayer—

> "For so the whole round earth is every way
> Bound by gold chains about the feet of God."

APPENDIX.

ADDITIONAL WELL-KNOWN HYMNS, WITH THEIR AUTHORS.

APPENDIX.

ADDITIONAL WELL-KNOWN HYMNS, WITH THEIR AUTHORS.

> "Christian, dost thou see them
> On the holy ground."
> *(Ancient & Mod.* **91**; *Church Hymns* **104**)

from the Greek of S. Andrew of Crete, translated by J. M. Neale, *Hymns of the Eastern Church*, 1862. S. Andrew was born at Damascus, about 660 A.D. and became Archbishop of Crete.

> "My God, I love Thee; not because
> I hope for heaven thereby."
> *(Ancient & Mod.* **106**; *Church Hymns* **434**)

from the Latin of Francis Xavier—

> O Deus, ego amo Te,
> Nec amo Te, ut salves me.

(Daniel, *Thesaurus Hymnol.* ii. 335) translated by Edward Caswall (see page 250). Xavier, the great Jesuit missionary, was born in Navarre in 1506, and died in the island of Sancian, near Macao, in China at the age of forty-five.

> "O Lord, turn not Thy face away,
> From them that lowly lie."
> (*Ancient & Mod.* 93; *Church Hymns* 111; *Hymnal Comp.* 120)

by John Marckant (not by John Mardley), author of *Verses to Divers Good Purposes*, 1580. The hymn—the "Humble Lamentation of a Sinner"—was appended to the first edition of the Old Version of the Psalms, 1562; it was altered, beginning as above, by Bishop Heber. At the end of the New Version, it begins—

> "O Lord, turn not Thy face from me
> Who lie in woeful state."

and is so generally given.

> "Jerusalem on high
> My song and city is."
> (*Ancient & Mod.* 233; *Church Hymns* 394; *Hymnal Comp.* 363)

part of a poem beginning—

> "Sweet place, sweet place alone,
> The court of God most High."

written by Samuel Crossman, a Canon of Bristol Cathedral, born in 1624: this first appeared in *The Young Man's Meditation, or Some few Sacred Poems*, 1664. Crossman was buried in the south aisle of Bristol Cathedral in 1683.

> "Come gracious Spirit, heavenly Dove,
> With light and comfort from above."
> *(Ancient & Mod. 209; Hymnal Comp. 245)*

an altered form of a hymn of seven verses—

> "Come, Holy Spirit, heavenly Dove."

written by Simon Browne in *Hymns and Spiritual Songs*, 1720. He was born at Shepton Mallet in Somersetshire in 1680, and became minister of the Independent Chapel in Old Jewry, London.

> "Awake, and sing the song
> Of Moses and the Lamb."
> *(Church Hymns 335; Hymnal Comp. 504)*

by William Hammond, born in 1719. After taking his degree at S. John's College, Cambridge, he became a preacher among the Calvinistic Methodists, and later joined the Moravian Brethren. The hymn appeared in his *Psalms, Hymns, and Spiritual Songs and Discourses*, 1745. It was altered by Martin Madan, 1760; the fifth verse is from a hymn by Watts. Hammond died in London in 1783.

> "Christians, awake, salute the happy morn,
> Whereon the Saviour of the world was born."
> *(Ancient & Mod. 61; Church Hymns 77; Hymnal Comp. 76)*

by John Byrom, born near Manchester in 1691. He became Fellow of Trinity College, Cambridge, and Fellow of the Royal Society. He wrote many poems, one of which was inserted in *The Spectator* for October 6, 1714. The hymn was not published until after his death in 1763. He is said to have refused to "revise and polish" Bishop Ken's poems in these words—

> "Patchwork improvements in the modern style,
> Bestowed upon some venerable pile,
> Do but deface it; poems to revise
> That Ken hath writ—another Ken must rise."

> "Who are these, like stars appearing,
> These, before God's Throne who stand?"
> (*Ancient & Mod.* 427; *Church Hymns* 554; *Hymnal Comp.* 360)

from the German of Heinrich Theobald Schenk—

> Wer sind die vor Gottes Throne.

He was master of a school, at Giessen in Hesse, and died in 1727. The translation is by Miss Frances E. Cox, *Sacred Hymns from the German*, 1841.

> "Jesus lives; no longer now
> Can thy terrors, Death, appal us."
> (*Ancient & Mod.* 140; *Church Hymns* 405; *Hymnal Comp.* 185)

from the German of Christian Fürchtegott Gellert—

> Jesus lebt, mit Ihm auch ich.

which appeared in his *Geistliche Lieder und Oden*, 1757. He was born in Saxony in 1715, and became Professor of Poetry and Philosophy at Leipsic. This translation is also by Miss Frances E. Cox, 1841.

> "Hail, Thou once despised Jesus,
> Hail, Thou Galilean King."
> *(Church Hymns* 378; *Hymnal Comp.* 175)

by John Bakewell, one of the earliest of the Wesleyan local preachers, and a friend of the Wesleys, Toplady, and Olivers. At his house, Olivers is said to have composed his 'Hymn to the God of Abraham' (see p. 150 and Sedgwick's edition of Olivers). Bakewell died at Lewisham in 1819, at the age of ninety-eight. The hymn is found in Madan's Collection, 1760; but it is said to have been published with others in 1757.

> "Far from these narrow scenes of night,
> Unbounded glories rise."
> *(Hymnal Comp.* 231)

by Anne Steele, born in 1716, the daughter of a Baptist minister, at Broughton in Hampshire, where she died in 1778. This hymn appeared in her *Poems on Subjects chiefly Devotional*, 1760; likewise the hymns—

> "Father of mercies, in Thy word
> What endless glory shines."
> *(Hymnal Comp.* 261)

and—

> "Father, whate'er of earthly bliss
> Thy sovereign will denies."
> *(Hymnal Comp.* 277)

This hymn forms the last three stanzas (of ten) of a hymn beginning—

["When

"When I survey life's varied scene,"
the first line reads—

"And O, whate'er of earthly bliss."

> "Praise to God, immortal praise,
> For the love that crowns our days."
> *(Church Hymns* 280; *Hymnal Comp.* 47)

by the well-known Anna Letitia Barbauld, who was born at Kibworth in Leicestershire in 1743. She was the daughter of Dr John Aikin, and the wife of a Unitarian minister, and died in 1825. The hymn appeared in her *Poems,* published in 1773. She is also the author of—

> "Again the Lord of life and light
> Awakes the kindling ray."
> *(Hymnal Comp.* 184)

> "Sweet the moments, rich in blessing,
> Which before the Cross I spend."
> *(Ancient & Mod.* 109; *Church Hymns* 506; *Hymnal Comp.* 171)

an altered form, written in 1770, by Hon. and Rev. Walter Shirley, a relative of the Countess of Huntingdon, of part of a hymn by James Allen beginning—

> "While my Jesus I'm possessing."

This latter appeared in what was known as *The Kendal Hymn Book,* 1757, of which Allen was the editor. The title was—*A Collection of Hymns, for the use of those that seek and those that have Redemption in the Blood of Christ.* In the copy that I have seen, the Preface is signed J. A.; C. B. (i.e. Christopher Batty). Allen, who was born in Wensleydale in 1734, became one of Lady Huntingdon's preachers, and afterwards a preacher on his own account in Yorkshire, and died in 1804.

"Guide me, O Thou great Jehovah,
Pilgrim through this barren land."
(*Ancient & Mod.* 196; *Church Hymns* 376; *Hymnal Comp.* 329)

from the Welsh of William Williams. He was born near Llandovery in Caermarthenshire in 1717; after being ordained deacon, he joined the Welsh Calvinistic Methodists, among whom he was a noted preacher, and died in 1791. The first verse, as translated by Rev. Peter Williams, was adopted by the author who completed the four English stanzas in 1774. The fourth stanza runs thus—

"Musing on my habitation,
Musing on my heavenly home,
Fills my soul with holy longing.
Come, my Jesus, quickly come.
Vanity is all I see,
Lord, I long to be with Thee."

He also wrote the Missionary hymn—

"O'er the gloomy hills of darkness,
Look, my soul, be still and gaze."
(*Hymnal Comp.* 107)

> "Spirit of mercy, truth and love,
> O shed Thine influence from above."
> <small>(Ancient & Mod. 155; Church Hymns 151; Hymnal Comp. 241)</small>

by an unknown writer. It is found as far back as 1774 in the Collection of hymns used at the Foundling Hospital.

> "All hail the power of Jesus' Name!
> Let angels prostrate fall."
> <small>(Ancient & Mod. 300; Church Hymns 330; Hymnal Comp. 499)</small>

by Edward Perronet, a friend of the Wesleys, and for a time one of their preachers; later a preacher in Lady Huntingdon's connexion. He died at Canterbury in 1792. The hymn appeared in the *Gospel Magazine* in 1780. The well-known tune "Miles' Lane" was written for it by William Shrubsole, organist of Spafields Chapel, London.

> "O Thou, from Whom all goodness flows,
> I lift my soul to Thee."
> <small>(Ancient & Mod. 283; Church Hymns 459; Hymnal Comp. 124)</small>

by Thomas Haweis, published in 1792. He was born in 1734, at Truro; after being a physician, he became Rector of Aldwinkle in Northamptonshire, and chaplain to Lady Huntingdon, and died in 1820. He is also the author of—

["Behold

> "Behold the Lamb of God, Who bore
> Thy burdens on the Tree."
> *(Hymnal Comp. 163)*

and—

> "The happy morn is come;
> Triumphant o'er the grave."
> *(Hymnal Comp. 177)*

> "Lord, dismiss us with Thy blessing,
> Fill our hearts with joy and peace."
> *(Church Hymns 51; Hymnal Comp. 215)*

by Rev. John Fawcett, a Baptist minister, who was born near Bradford in Yorkshire, and died in 1817. He published a book of hymns in 1782; but the authorship of this hymn has been much discussed. It is found, with his name attached, in Hymn Books of the last century.

> "Lo, round the Throne, a glorious band,
> The Saints in countless myriads stand."
> *(Ancient & Mod. 435)*

sometimes written—

> "Lo, round the Throne, at God's right hand."
> *(Hymnal Comp. 362)*

is founded on a hymn by the well-known Rev. Rowland Hill beginning—

> "Exalted high, at God's right hand."

[(see

(see *The Book of Praise*, cxii.) The hymn is in Thomas Cotterill's *Selection*, 1819, and was, probably, altered by him in common with so many others. Rowland Hill published his chief *Collection of Psalms and Hymns* in 1783; and died in 1833, at the age of ninety-nine.

> "O let him, whose sorrow
> No relief can find."
> (*Ancient & Mod.* 286; *Church Hymns* 471)

from the German—

> Wenn in Leidenstagen.

by Heinrich Sigismund Oswald, who was born in Silesia in 1751, and became a Prussian privy councillor. The translation is by Miss Frances E. Cox, *Sacred Hymns from the German*, 1841.

> "Fountain of mercy, God of love,
> How rich Thy bounties are."
> (*Hymnal Comp.* 50)

in some Hymnals this begins—

> "Father of mercies, God of love."
> (*Ancient & Mod.* 388)

written by Alice Flowerdew, who died in 1830. She was the widow of a government official in Jamaica, and kept a school in London. The hymn appeared in an edition of her *Poems* published in 1811.

> "Come, ye faithful, raise the anthem,
> Cleave the skies with shouts of praise."
> (*Ancient & Mod.* 302; *Church Hymns*.352)

altered by J. M. Neale from a hymn, of thirteen stanzas, by Job Hupton beginning—

> "Come, ye saints, and raise an anthem."

Hupton was one of Lady Huntingdon's itinerant preachers, afterwards a Baptist Minister in Norfolk; he died in 1849, at the age of eighty-eight.

> " Hail, Thou Source of every blessing,
> Sovereign Father of mankind."
> (*Church Hymns* 96; *Hymnal Comp.* 95)

by Rev. Basil Woodd, born in 1760, for many years preacher at S. Peter's, Cornhill, and Bentinck Chapel, Marylebone. He was one of the many who have published a *Metrical Version of the Psalms*, in which this and other hymns appeared in 1801. He died in 1831.

> " Father of heaven, Whose love profound
> A ransom for our souls hath found."
> (*Ancient & Mod.* 164; *Church Hymns* 359; *Hymnal Comp.* 254)

by Rev. Edward Cooper, the Rector of a parish in Staffordshire, who died in 1833. The hymn appears in Collections as early as 1808.

> "Praise the Lord! ye heavens, adore Him,
> Praise Him, Angels, in the height."
> *(Ancient & Mod. 292; Church Hymns 486; Hymnal Comp. 524)*

This fine paraphrase of Psalm cxlviii. is ascribed to Rev. John Kempthorne, Rector of S. Michael's, Gloucester, where he died in 1838. It is ascribed to him mainly on the ground that it appeared in a Collection published by him—*Select Portions of Psalms and Hymns*, 1810.

> "Lead us, heavenly Father, lead us
> O'er the world's tempestuous sea."
> *(Ancient & Mod. 281; Church Hymns 410; Hymnal Comp. 330)*

by James Edmeston, a London architect, who died in 1867. He wrote a very large number of hymns. The above appeared in his *Sacred Lyrics*, 1821. He is also the author of—

> "Saviour, breathe an evening blessing,
> Ere repose our spirits seal."
> *(Church Hymns 28; Hymnal Comp. 23)*

> "Father, again in Jesus' Name we meet,
> And bow in penitence beneath Thy feet."
> *(Church Hymns 105; Hymnal Comp. 14)*

by Lady Lucy Whitmore, who died in 1840. This is one of the hymns in a book of *Family Prayers* which she published in 1824.

"Thou art the Way;—to Thee alone
From sin and death we flee."
(Ancient & Mod. 199; Church Hymns 526; Hymnal Comp. 306)

by the American Bishop, George Washington Doane, D.D., Bishop of New Jersey, who died in 1859. This hymn appeared in his *Songs by the Way*, 1824.

"O for a faith that will not shrink,
Though pressed by many a foe."
(Ancient & Mod. 278; Hymnal Comp. 265)

by Rev. William Hiley Bathurst, for many years Rector of Barwick-in-Elmet, near Leeds, who died in 1877. This hymn appeared in his *Psalms and Hymns for Public and Private Use*, 1831. Also—

"O Saviour, may we never rest
Till Thou art formed within."
(Hymnal Comp. 307)

"Take up thy cross, the Saviour said,
If thou would'st My disciple be."
(Ancient & Mod. 263; Church Hymns 507; Hymnal Comp. 309)

by the American writer, Rev. Charles William Everest, who died in 1877. The hymn appeared in his *Visions of Death and other Poems*, 1833.

"Bread of heaven, on Thee we feed,
For Thy flesh is meat indeed."
(Ancient & Mod. 318; Church Hymns 203; Hymnal Comp. 388)

[by

by Josiah Conder, a publisher and the first editor of *The Congregational Hymn Book*, 1836. He was born in London, in 1789, and was a most prolific writer, and died in 1855. He is also the author of—

"The Lord is King, lift up thy voice,
O earth, and all ye heavens, rejoice."
(*Church Hymns* 513)

"O God, unseen, yet ever near,
Thy presence may we feel."
(*Ancient & Mod.* 320; *Church Hymns* 213; *Hymnal Comp.* 384)

by Edward Osler, who was born at Falmouth in 1798, and brought up a dissenter, but who afterwards joined the Church of England. He was at first a surgeon, and then devoted himself to literary work. The hymn first appeared in Hall's 'Mitre' *Hymn Book*, 1836, to which he was a large contributor. He died at Truro in 1863. See also page 123.

"O Lord, how happy should we be,
If we could cast our care on Thee."
(*Ancient & Mod.* 276; *Church Hymns* 452; *Hymnal Comp.* 469)

by Joseph Anstice, who took a very high degree at Oxford, and became Student of Christ Church. He was made Professor of Classics in King's College, London; but died, before he was thirty years of age, in 1836. His hymns were printed privately very shortly after his death; some of them were published in *The Child's Christian Year*, 1841. Among them are—

"Father, by Thy love and power
Comes again the evening hour."
(Church Hymns 20; Hymnal Comp. 31)

and—

"Lord of the harvest, once again
We thank Thee for the ripened grain."
(Ancient & Mod. 387)

"Lord, as to Thy dear Cross we flee,
And plead to be forgiven."
(Ancient & Mod. 267; Hymnal Comp. 303)

by Rev. John Hampden Gurney, Rector of S. Mary's, Marylebone, and Prebendary of S. Paul's, who died in 1862. This hymn appeared in his Collection of *Hymns for Public Worship*, 1838. He is also the author of the Children's hymn—

"Fair waved the golden corn
In Canaan's pleasant land."
(Ancient & Mod. 339; Church Hymns 569; Hymnal Comp. 426)

"Great King of nations, hear our prayer,
While at Thy feet we fall."
Ancient & Mod. 375; Church Hymns 259; Hymnal Comp. 38)

"Lord of the harvest, Thee we hail;
Thine ancient promise doth not fail."
(Church Hymns 279; Hymnal Comp. 49)

["We

> "We saw Thee not when Thou didst come
> To this poor world of sin and death."
>
> *(Ancient & Mod. 174; Church Hymns 541; Hymnal Comp. 268)*

and—

> "Yes, God is good; in earth and sky,
> From ocean depths and spreading wood."
>
> *(Hymnal Comp. 435)*

> "Nearer, my God, to Thee,
> Nearer to Thee."
>
> *(Ancient & Mod. 277; Church Hymns 437; Hymnal Comp. 312)*

by Sarah Adams, born at Cambridge in 1805, the daughter of Benjamin Flower, editor of *The Cambridge Intelligencer*. She was a Unitarian, and died in 1848. This hymn, with others, appeared in 1841.

> "O come, all ye faithful,
> Joyful and triumphant."
>
> *(Ancient & Mod. 59; Church Hymns 85; Hymnal Comp. 77)*

from the Latin—

> Adeste fideles, læti triumphantes.

probably of the 17th or 18th century, said to have been taken from a *Gradual* of the Cistercian monks. The tune '*Adeste Fideles*' was written by John Reading (the latest of three musicians of the name), an organist in London, who died in 1764; it was also called 'The Portuguese Hymn' from its use at the Chapel of the Portuguese Embassy in London. The above hymn is altered from the translation (1841) by Rev. Frederick Oakeley, beginning—

"Ye faithful, approach ye."

He was formerly a Fellow of Balliol College, Oxford, and a Prebendary of Lichfield. Having joined the Church of Rome in 1845, he became a Canon of the pro-Cathedral, Westminster, and died in 1880. See also page 46.

"Above the clear blue sky,
In heaven's bright abode."
(Ancient & Mod. 336; Church Hymns 565)

This hymn for children is by Rev. John Chandler, to whose translations reference has been so often made (see especially page 125). He was a Fellow of Corpus Christi College, Oxford, then Vicar of Witley in Surrey, and died in 1876. Most of his renderings are to be found in his *Hymns of the Church, mostly Primitive,* 1841. Another, a hymn for the Ascension, is—

"Jesu (or "O Christ") our Hope, our heart's Desire,
Thy work of grace we sing."
(Ancient & Mod. 150)

from an ancient Latin hymn, ascribed to Ambrose or his school—

Jesu, nostra redemptio,
Amor et desiderium.

> "For Thy mercy and Thy grace,
> Faithful through another year."
>
> (*Ancient & Mod.* 73; *Church Hymns* 89; *Hymnal Comp.* 84)

by Rev. Henry Downton, Rector of Hopton, Suffolk, for many years chaplain at Geneva. The hymn first appeared in the *Church of England Magazine*, 1843. To him is also due the Missionary hymn—

> "Lord, her watch Thy Church is keeping,
> When shall earth Thy rule obey?"
>
> (*Ancient & Mod.* 362; *Church Hymns* 292; *Hymnal Comp.* 110)

> "Thine for ever! God of love,
> Hear us from Thy throne above."
>
> (*Ancient & Mod.* 280; *Church Hymns* 523; *Hymnal Comp.* 282)

by Mrs Mary Fawler Maude, wife of Rev. Joseph Maude, formerly Vicar of Chirk, near Ruabon. The hymn was written for a Confirmation class, and was published in 1848.

> "They come, God's messengers of love,
> They come from realms of peace above."
>
> (*Ancient & Mod.* 424; *Church Hymns* 521)

by Robert Campbell, an advocate in Edinburgh, who joined the Church of Rome, and died in 1868. Most of his hymns are translations from the Latin, and appeared in his *Hymns and Anthems*, 1850. Such are—

["At

> "At the Lamb's high feast we sing
> Praise to our victorious King."
> <small>(*Ancient & Mod.* 127; *Church Hymns* 128)</small>

from the Latin—

> Ad regias Agni dapes.

the Roman Breviary version of the ancient Ambrosian hymn—

> Ad cœnam Agni providi.

> "Come, pure hearts, in sweetest measures
> Sing of those who spread the treasures."
> <small>(*Ancient & Mod.* 434)</small>

founded on portions of two hymns of Adam of S. Victor—

> Jucundare plebs fidelis.

and—

> Psallat chorus corde mundo.

both given by Trench, *Sacred Latin Poetry*, p. 62. *seq*.

> "Ye choirs of New Jerusalem,
> Your sweetest notes employ."
> <small>(*Ancient & Mod.* 125)</small>

his translation from the hymn of Fulbert of Chartres, about 1000 A. D.—

> Chorus Novae Jerusalem.

[and—

and—

> "Ye servants of our glorious King,
> To Him your thankful praises bring."
> *(Ancient & Mod. 444)*

from a Latin hymn in the Roman Breviary—

> Christo profusum sanguinem.

a version of the Ambrosian hymn (see page 22)—

> Æterna Christi munera.

> "Three in One, and One in Three,
> Ruler of the earth and sea."
> *(Ancient & Mod. 163; Church Hymns 529; Hymnal Comp. 256)*

by Rev. Gilbert Rorison, LL.D., Incumbent of S. Peter's Episcopal Church, Peterhead, Aberdeen, who died there in 1869. The hymn was written for his congregation in 1850, and is evidently founded on the two very ancient Latin hymns—

> Tu, Trinitatis Unitas.

and—

> O Lux beata, Trinitas.

(see p. 20), or their adaptations in the Roman Breviary.

> "Lord, to whom except to Thee,
> Shall our wandering spirits go."
> *(Church Hymns 428; Hymnal Comp. 394)*

by Rev. John Samuel Bewley Monsell, LL.D., who was Rector of S. Nicholas', Guildford, and died there in 1875.

He was formerly examining chaplain to Bishop Mant, and was the author of several poetical works. This hymn appeared in *Parish Musings*, 1850; many of his others in *Hymns of Love and Praise for the Church's Year*, 1863. His also are—the hymn for Holy Baptism—

"God of that glorious gift of grace
By which Thy people seek Thy face."
(*Church Hymns* 222; *Hymnal Comp.* 398)

"Holy offerings, rich and rare,
Offerings of praise and prayer."
(*Church Hymns* 284)

"Mighty Father, Blessed Son,
Holy Spirit, Three in One."
(*Hymnal Comp.* 258)

"Rest of the weary, joy of the sad,
Hope of the dreary, light of the glad."
(*Hymnal Comp.* 339)

"Sinful, sighing to be blest,
Bound, and longing to be free."
(*Hymnal Comp.* 148)

and—

"Sing to the Lord a joyful song,
Lift up your hearts, your voices raise."
(*Church Hymns* 498)

"Saviour, sprinkle many nations,
Fruitful let Thy sorrows be."
(*Ancient & Mod.* 359; *Church Hymns* 294)

by Arthur Cleveland Coxe, D.D., consecrated Bishop of

Western New York in 1864. This hymn was written when on a visit to England in 1851. He is the author of many poetical and other works.

> "Thou art gone up on high
> To mansions in the skies."
> *(Ancient & Mod. 149 ; Church Hymns 525; Hymnal Comp. 224)*

by the late Emma Toke, wife of Rev. Nicholas Toke, and daughter of Bishop Leslie of Kilmore. This and other hymns were written in 1851 for the Collection of the Society for Promoting Christian Knowledge. To her also belongs—

> "Glory to Thee, O Lord,
> Who from this world of sin."
> *(Ancient & Mod. 69; Church Hymns 166; Hymnal Comp. 347)*

> "It came upon the midnight clear,
> That glorious song of old."
> *(Church Hymns 82; Hymnal Comp. 367)*

by Dr Edmund Hamilton Sears, an American Unitarian minister, who was born in Berkshire County, Massachusetts, in 1810, and died in 1876. This hymn was published in 1851 in the *Christian Register*.

> "Crown Him with many crowns,
> The Lamb upon His throne."
> *(Ancient & Mod. 304; Church Hymns 354; Hymnal Comp. 225)*

by Matthew Bridges, who joined the Roman Catholic Church in 1847. It appeared in a book of hymns, *The Passion of Jesus*, 1852. He is also the author of—

"Behold the Lamb!
O Thou for sinners slain."
(*Ancient & Mod.* 187; *Church Hymns* 336)

and the Confirmation hymn—

"My God, accept my heart this day,
And make it always Thine."
(*Ancient & Mod.* 349; *Church Hymns* 236)

"Jesu, my Lord, my God, my All,
Hear me, blest Saviour, when I call."
(*Ancient & Mod.* 191; *Church Hymns* 399; *Hymnal Comp.* 289)

by Rev. Henry Collins, who was ordained in the Church of England, and in 1857 joined the Church of Rome. This hymn was written in 1852. He also wrote—

"Jesu, meek and lowly,
Saviour, pure and holy."
(*Ancient & Mod.* 188; *Church Hymns* 398)

"In token that thou shalt not fear
Christ crucified to own."
(*Ancient & Mod.* 328; *Church Hymns* 227; *Hymnal Comp.* 400)

by the late Henry Alford, D.D., Dean of Canterbury, who died in 1871. The above was written in 1832, and, according to his *Life*, was first sung at the baptism of his eldest child in 1836; but this and most of his well-known hymns are to be found in his Collection entitled, *The Year of Praise*, 1867. He is also the author of—

"Come, ye thankful people, come,
Raise the song of Harvest home."
(*Ancient & Mod.* 382; *Church Hymns* 276; *Hymnal Comp.* 51)

"Forward! be our watchword,
Steps and voices joined."
(*Ancient & Mod.* 392; *Hymnal Comp.* 323)

"Lo, the storms of life are breaking;
Faithless fears our hearts are shaking."
(*Church Hymns* 268)

and—

"Ten thousand times ten thousand,
In sparkling raiment bright."
(*Ancient & Mod.* 222; *Hymnal Comp.* 72)

"We love the place, O God,
Wherein Thine honour dwells."
(*Ancient & Mod.* 242; *Church Hymns* 540; *Hymnal Comp.* 209)

by William Bullock, D.D., Dean of Nova Scotia. The hymn appeared in his *Songs of the Church*, 1854; but the last three verses in the above Hymnals are by Sir Henry Baker. He is also the author of the hymn—'In time of pestilence'—

"In grief and fear to Thee, O Lord,
We now for succour fly."
(Ancient & Mod. 377)

"Lord of our life and God of our salvation,
Star of our night, and Hope of every nation."
(Ancient & Mod. 214; Church Hymns 269)

by Philip Pusey, who was the elder brother of the well-known Dr Pusey and died in 1855. The hymn was published in the *Salisbury Hymn Book* in 1857, and is founded on the fine hymn of Matthäus Apelles von Löwenstern—

Christe, Du Beistand Deiner Kreuzgemeine.

written during the Thirty Years' War. See Bunsen, *Gesangbuch*, No. 300.

"How blessed, from the bonds of sin
And earthly fetters free."
(Ancient & Mod. 357; Church Hymns 300)

This hymn for Church workers is by Miss Jane Borthwick, joint author with her sister, Mrs Findlater, of *Hymns from the Land of Luther* (1st series, 1854), whence their frequent signature, H. L. L. Hers also is the hymn—

> "Come, labour on,
> Who dares stand idle on the harvest plain."
> *(Hymnal Comp. 315)*

published in *Thoughts for Thoughtful Hours*, 1859.

Of their excellent translations from the German, one has been already mentioned (page 133). Others are—

> "Rejoice, all ye believers,
> And let your lights appear."
> *(Hymnal Comp. 70)*

from the German of Laurentius Laurenti, who died in 1722—

> Ermuntert euch, ihr Frommen.

And—

> "Jesu, Sun of Righteousness,
> Brightest beam of love Divine."
> *(Hymnal Comp. 7)*

from the German of Knorr von Rosenroth, who died in 1689—

> Morgenglanz der Ewigkeit.

> "O Jesu, Thou art standing
> Outside the fast-closed door."
> *(Ancient & Mod. 198; Church Hymns 451; Hymnal Comp. 156)*

by William Walsham How, D.D., the present Bishop of Bedford. The hymn appeared first in the Collection of which he was one of the compilers in 1854. He also wrote—

"For all the Saints who from their labours rest,
Who Thee by faith before the world confessed."
(Ancient & Mod. 437; Church Hymns 196; Hymnal Comp. 354)

"Jesus, Name of wondrous love,
Name all other names above."
(Church Hymns 406)

"O Word of God Incarnate,
O Wisdom from on high."
(Church Hymns 462; Hymnal Comp. 263)

"To Thee, our God, we fly
For mercy and for grace."
(Ancient & Mod. 142; Church Hymns 537)

"We give Thee but Thine own,
Whate'er the gift may be."
(Ancient & Mod. 366; Church Hymns 287; Hymnal Comp. 373)

and—

"Who is this, so weak and helpless,
Child of lowly Hebrew maid."
(Church Hymns 555; Hymnal Comp. 81)

"O quickly come, dread Judge of all;
For, awful though Thine advent be."
(Ancient & Mod. 204; Church Hymns 474; Hymnal Comp. 60)

by Rev. Lawrence Tuttiett, Incumbent of the Episcopal Church of S. Andrew's, N.B. The hymn appeared in Morrell and How's *Psalms and Hymns*, 1854. He also wrote the New Year's Day hymn—

> "Father, let me dedicate
> All this year to Thee."
> *(Ancient & Mod. 74)*

the Confirmation hymn—

> "Go forward, Christian soldier,
> Beneath His banner true."
> *(Church Hymns 235)*

the hymn 'After Baptism'—

> "No sign we ask from heaven above,
> Nor rushing wind, nor hovering Dove."
> *(Church Hymns 226)*

and—

> "O Jesu, ever present,
> O Shepherd, ever kind."
> *(Church Hymns 449)*

> "O Love, Who formedst me to wear
> The image of Thy Godhead here."
> *(Ancient & Mod. 192; Church Hymns 456)*

by Miss Catherine Winkworth, several of whose translations from the German have been already mentioned. Most of them appeared in *Lyra Germanica* (1st series 1855; 2nd series 1858). She died in 1878. This hymn is a translation of—

> Liebe, die Du mich zum Bilde.

written in 1657 by Angelus Silesius—the name adopted by Johann Scheffler, born at Breslau in Silesia in 1624; he was a Protestant physician who afterwards became a

Jesuit priest. Some of his hymns were translated by John Wesley (see page 137). Miss Winkworth also wrote—

> "Christ the Lord is risen again;
> Christ hath broken every chain."
> *(Ancient & Mod. 136; Church Hymns 133)*

from the German—

> Christus ist erstanden
> Von des Todes Banden.

written by Michael Weiss, one of the early German pastors of the Bohemian brethren at Fulnek (see page 130). He translated many of the Bohemian hymns and died in 1540. This first appeared in German in a hymn book published for the Brethren in 1531.

> "O Father, Thou (original "Heart") Who hast created all
> In wisest love, we pray."
> *(Ancient & Mod. 325)*

a translation from—

> O Vaterherz, das Erd und Himmel schuf.

written for the baptism of his children by Albert Knapp, an Evangelical minister in Stuttgard, who died in 1864.

and—

> "Tender (original "Gentle") Shepherd, Thou hast stilled
> Now Thy little lamb's long weeping."
> *(Ancient & Mod. 402; Church Hymns 249; Hymnal Comp. 485)*

[from the

from the German—

> Guter Hirt, Du hast gestillt.

by Johann Wilhelm Meinhold, long a Lutheran pastor in Pomerania, who died in 1851.

> "Days and moments quickly flying
> Speed us onward to the dead."
> (*Ancient & Mod.* 289; *Church Hymns* 88; *Hymnal Comp.* 85)

by Rev. Edward Caswall, who in 1847 joined the Roman Catholic Church, and died in 1878. Many of his admirable translations have been before noted (see especially pages 37—41); most of these were published in his *Lyra Catholica*, 1849. The above hymn appeared in *The Masque of Mary and other Poems*, 1858. He is also the author of the Whitsuntide hymn—

> "Above the starry spheres,
> To where He was before."
> (*Ancient & Mod.* 152)

from the old Ambrosian hymn—

> Jam Christus astra ascenderat.

> "All ye who seek for sure relief
> In trouble and distress."
> (*Ancient & Mod.* 112)

from the Latin—

> Quicunque certum quæritis.

in the Roman *Breviarium Minorum* (1757).

> "Glory be to Jesus,
> Who in bitter pains."
> *(Ancient & Mod.* 107; *Church Hymns* 369)

taken from the Italian—"*Viva! Viva! Gesù*"—probably of the 18th century.

> "The sun is sinking fast,
> The daylight dies."
> *(Ancient & Mod.* 17; *Hymnal Comp.* 20)

> "When morning gilds the skies
> My heart awaking cries."
> *(Ancient & Mod.* 303)

and the two Passion hymns—

> "He Who once in righteous vengeance."
> *(Ancient & Mod.* 102)

and—

> "O'erwhelmed in depths of woe."
> *(Ancient & Mod.* 101)

from two hymns in the Roman Breviary, *Ira justa Conditoris* and *Sævo dolorem turbine*.

> "Jesu, meek and gentle,
> Son of God most High."
> *(Ancient & Mod.* 194; *Church Hymns* 397; *Hymnal Comp.* 423)

by Rev. George Rundle Prynne, Vicar of St Peter's,

Plymouth. This hymn appeared in a *Hymnal* published by him in 1858.

> "I need Thee, precious Jesu,
> For I am full of sin."
> *(Hymnal Comp.* **145**)

by Rev. Frederick Whitfield; Vicar of St Mary's, Hastings. This hymn was published in his *Sacred Poems and Prose,* 1859; also—

> "There is a Name I love to hear,
> I love to sing its worth."
> *(Hymnal Comp.* **291**)

> "There is a blessed home
> Beyond this land of woe."
> *(Ancient & Mod.* **230**; *Church Hymns* **517**; *Hymnal Comp.* **233**)

by the late Sir Henry Williams Baker, Bart., Vicar of Monkland, Herefordshire, and Chairman of the Committee of *Hymns Ancient and Modern.* For that Hymnal (1st edition, 1861) most of his hymns and translations were written. Some have been already mentioned; others are—

> "From highest heaven, the eternal Son,
> With God the Father ever One."
> *(Ancient & Mod.* **171**)

Appendix.

"Lord, Thy Word abideth,
And our footsteps guideth."
(Ancient & Mod. 243; *Church Hymns* 426)

"O what, if we are Christ's,
Is earthly shame and loss."
(Ancient & Mod. 446)

"Out of the deep I call
To Thee, O Lord, to Thee."
(Ancient & Mod. 250; *Church Hymns* 482)

"Rejoice to-day with one accord,
Sing out with exultation."
(Ancient & Mod. 378; *Hymnal Comp.* 53)

"The King of love my Shepherd is,
Whose goodness faileth never."
(Ancient & Mod. 197; *Church Hymns* 512; *Hymnal Comp.* 395)

Two lines of this hymn were the last words uttered by the author just before his death in 1877—

"And on His shoulder gently laid,
And home, rejoicing, brought me."

"'Tis done! that new and heavenly birth,
Which recreates the sons of earth."
(Ancient & Mod. 327)

and the translation—

"What our Father does is well,
Blessed truth His children tell."
(Ancient & Mod. 389; *Church Hymns* 267)

from the German hymn—

Was Gott thut, das ist wohlgethan.

by Benjamin Schmolck, a pastor and prolific hymnwriter in Schweidnitz, Silesia, who died there in 1737.

"Eternal Father, strong to save,
Whose arm doth bind the restless wave."
(Ancient & Mod. 370; Church Hymns 321; Hymnal Comp. 533)

This hymn, 'For those at Sea,' which, with Dykes' tune *Melita*, is so popular, was written by William Whiting, long Master of Winchester College Choristers' School, who died in 1878. It appeared in the first edition of *Hymns Ancient and Modern*, 1861.

"As with gladness men of old
Did the guiding star behold."
(Ancient & Mod. 79; Church Hymns 94; Hymnal Comp. 93)

by William Chatterton Dix, born at Bristol in 1837. The hymn appeared in the first edition of *Hymns Ancient and Modern*, 1861. He has written many other hymns, among them—

"Alleluia! sing to Jesus!
His the Sceptre, His the Throne."
(Ancient & Mod. 316; Church Hymns 332)

being No. vii. of his *Altar Songs*, 1867.

"Come unto Me, ye weary,
And I will give you rest."
(Ancient & Mod. 256; Church Hymns 351; Hymnal Comp. 345)

"Joy fills our inmost heart to-day,
The royal Child is born."
(Church Hymns 83; Hymnal Comp. 79)

"On the waters dark and drear,
Jesus, Saviour, Thou art near."
(Ancient & Mod. 372; Church Hymns 325)

and—

"To Thee, O Lord, our hearts we raise
In hymns of adoration."
(Ancient & Mod. 384; Church Hymns 281)

"We plough the fields, and scatter
The good seed on the land."
(Ancient & Mod. 383; Church Hymns 282)

This Harvest hymn is by Miss Jane Montgomery Campbell, and appeared in *A Garland of Songs*, 1861, edited by Rev. C. S. Bere. It is from the German—

Wir pflügen und wir streuen.

by Matthias Claudius, who was born in Schleswig-Holstein in 1740, and died in 1815. The hymn appeared in a tale written by him—*Paul Erdmann's Fest*, in 1782.

> "Hark, the sound of holy voices,
> Chanting at the crystal Sea."
> *(Ancient & Mod. 436; Church Hymns 199; Hymnal Comp. 370)*

by Christopher Wordsworth, D.D., late Bishop of Lincoln, who died in 1885. His hymns appeared in *The Holy Year* (1st edition, 1862). Others by him are—

> "Alleluia! Alleluia! Hearts to heaven and voices raise."
> *(Ancient & Mod. 137; Church Hymns 127; Hymnal Comp. 187)*

> "Father of all, from land and sea
> The nations sing, 'Thine, Lord, are we'."
> *(Ancient & Mod. 275)*

> "Gracious Spirit, Holy Ghost,
> Taught by Thee, we covet most."
> *(Ancient & Mod. 210; Church Hymns 374)*

> "O day of rest and gladness,
> O day of joy and light."
> *(Ancient & Mod. 36; Church Hymns 45; Hymnal Comp. 191)*

> "O Lord of heaven and earth and sea,
> To Thee all praise and glory be."
> *(Ancient & Mod. 365; Church Hymns 285; Hymnal Comp. 372)*

> "See the Conqueror mounts in triumph,
> See the King in royal state."
> *(Ancient & Mod. 148; Church Hymns 147; Hymnal Comp. 222)*

> "Songs of thankfulness and praise,
> Jesu, Lord, to Thee we raise."
> *(Ancient & Mod. 81; Church Hymns 100)*

and—

"When the Architect Almighty had created heaven
and earth."
(*Church Hymns* 310)

"From all Thy saints in warfare, for all Thy saints at rest,
To Thee, O Blessed Jesu, all praises be addressed."
(*Church Hymns* 157; *Hymnal Comp.* 353)

by Earl Nelson. It first appeared in *Hymns for Saints' Days, and other Hymns, by a Layman*, 1864, afterwards in *The Sarum Hymnal*, 1868.

"Thine arm, O Lord, in days of old
Was strong to heal and save."
(*Ancient & Mod.* 369; *Church Hymns* 298)

by Edward Hayes Plumptre, D.D., Dean of Wells. The hymn was written for the Chapel of King's College Hospital, London, in 1865. He is also the author of—

"O Light, Whose beams illumine all
From twilight dawn to perfect day."
(*Ancient & Mod.* 345)

and—

"Rejoice, ye pure in heart,
Rejoice, give thanks and sing."
(*Ancient & Mod.* 393; *Church Hymns* 489)

> "And now the wants are told, that brought
> Thy children to Thy knee."
> *(Ancient & Mod. 32)*

by William Bright, D.D., Canon of Christ Church and Professor of Ecclesiastical History, Oxford. This and some of his other hymns were published in *Hymns and Verses*, 1866. He wrote the Confirmation hymn—

> "Behold us, Lord, before Thee met
> Whom each bright angel serves and fears."
> *(Ancient & Mod. 348; Church Hymns 232)*

also the two hymns for Holy Communion—

> "And now, O Father, mindful of the love
> That bought us, once for all, on Calvary's Tree."
> *(Ancient & Mod. 322)*

and—

> "Once, only once, and once for all,
> His precious life He gave."
> *(Ancient & Mod. 315)*

> "O Jesu, I have promised
> To serve Thee to the end."
> *(Ancient & Mod. 271; Church Hymns 450; Hymnal Comp. 451)*

by Rev. John Ernest Bode, Student of Christ Church, Oxford, and Rector of Castle Camps, Cambridgeshire, where he died in 1874. This hymn was written in 1869 for the Confirmation of his son, who died in 1885.

> "Almighty Father, hear our cry,
> As o'er the trackless deep we roam."
> *(Ancient & Mod. 371; Hymnal Comp. 532)*

This well-known 'Hymn to be used at Sea', is by Edward Henry Bickersteth, D.D., the present Bishop of Exeter. Several of his hymns, although published previously, are included in his *Hymnal Companion to the Book of Common Prayer* (1st edition, 1870). Among them the Missionary hymn—

> "O brothers, lift your voices,
> Triumphant songs to raise."
> *(Hymnal Comp. 114)*

a beautiful hymn for the close of the year—

> "O God, the Rock of Ages,
> Who evermore hast been."
> *(Hymnal Comp. 83)*

and another for the close of the day—

> "Peace, perfect peace, in this dark world of sin?
> The blood of Jesus whispers peace within."
> *(Hymnal Comp. 32)*

> "The Saints of God, their conflict past,
> And life's long battle won at last."
> *(Ancient & Mod. 428; Church Hymns 191)*

by William Dalrymple Maclagan, D.D., the present Bishop of Lichfield. He is also the author of the two

Passion hymns—

> "It is finished! Blessed Jesus,
> Thou hast breathed Thy latest sigh."
> *(Ancient & Mod. 122)*

and—

> "Lord, when Thy Kingdom comes, remember me."
> *(Ancient & Mod. 116)*

> "The strife is o'er, the battle done,
> The victory of life is won."
> *(Ancient & Mod. 135; Church Hymns 139; Hymnal Comp. 180)*

by Rev. Francis Pott, Rector of Norhill, Bedfordshire, founded on a Latin hymn, probably of the 12th century—

> Finita jam sunt prælia.

He is also the author of—

> "The year is gone beyond recall,
> 'Tis gone—with all its hopes and fears."
> *(Ancient & Mod. 72; Church Hymns 93)*

from a Latin hymn in the *Meaux Breviary*—

> Lapsus est annus; redit annus alter.

> "Saviour, again to Thy dear Name we raise
> With one accord our parting hymn of praise."
> *(Ancient & Mod. 31; Church Hymns 27; Hymnal Comp. 214)*

by Rev. John Ellerton, Rector of Barnes, author of many beautiful hymns, which have appeared in various

Appendix.

Hymnals, as—

> "Joy! because the circling year
> Brings our day of blessings here."
> *(Ancient & Mod.* 153; *Church Hymns* 149)

from the Latin hymn, probably of the 7th century—

> Beata nobis gaudia.

> "Lift the strain of high thanksgiving!
> Tread with songs the hallowed way."
> *(Ancient & Mod.* 397; *Church Hymns* 311)

> "Now the labourer's task is o'er;
> Now the battle day is past."
> *(Ancient & Mod.* 401; *Church Hymns* 247; *Hymnal Comp.* 482)

> "O Strength and Stay upholding all creation,
> Who ever dost Thyself unmoved abide."
> *(Ancient & Mod.* 12; *Church Hymns* 15)

from the Ambrosian Latin hymn—

> Rerum Deus tenax vigor.

> "Our day of praise is done;
> The evening shadows fall."
> *(Ancient & Mod.* 30; *Church Hymns* 42; *Hymnal Comp.* 197)

> "This is the day of Light;
> Let there be light to day."
> *(Ancient & Mod.* 37; *Church Hymns* 47; *Hymnal Comp.* 189)

and—

> "Welcome, happy morning! age to age shall say."
> *(Church Hymns* 131; *Hymnal Comp.* 179)

from the Easter hymn of Venantius Fortunatus (see

page 28)—
> Salve festa dies, toto venerabilis ævo.

> " Saviour, Blessed Saviour,
>   Listen whilst we sing."
> *(Ancient & Mod.* 305; *Church Hymns* 493; *Hymnal Comp.* 342)

by Rev. Godfrey Thring, Rector of Alford with Hornblotton, Somersetshire, and Prebendary of Wells. An excellent Hymnal, *The Church of England Hymn Book* (new edition), was published by him in 1882. To him are also due—

> " Fierce raged the tempest o'er the deep,
>   Watch did Thine anxious servants keep."
> *(Ancient & Mod.* 285; *Hymnal Comp.* 535)

> "The radiant morn hath passed away,
>   And spent too soon her golden store."
> *(Ancient & Mod.* 19; *Church Hymns* 16)

and—

> " Thou, to Whom, the sick and dying
>   Ever came, nor came in vain."
> *(Ancient & Mod.* 368; *Church Hymns* 302)

> " At even, ere the sun was set,
>   The sick, O Lord, around Thee lay."
> *(Ancient & Mod.* 20; *Church Hymns* 18; *Hymnal Comp.* 19)

by Rev. Henry Twells, Rector of Waltham, Leicestershire. The hymn first appeared in *Hymns Ancient and Modern,* 1868.

INDEX OF HYMNS.

	PAGE
A few more years shall roll	210
A hymn for martyrs sweetly sing	31
A living stream, as crystal clear	197
A sure stronghold our God is He	64
Abide with me; fast falls the eventide	199
Above the clear blue sky	237
Above the starry spheres	250
According to Thy gracious word	172
Again the Lord of life and light	226
All glory, laud and honour	34
All hail the power of Jesus' Name	228
All people that on earth do dwell	76
All praise to Thee, my God, this night	103
All ye who seek for sure relief	250
Alleluia! Alleluia! hearts to heaven and voices raise	256
Alleluia! sing to Jesus	254
Alleluia! song of sweetness	60
Almighty Father, hear our cry	259
And now, O Father, mindful of the love	258
And now the wants are told that brought	258
Angels from the realms of glory	172
Approach, my soul, the mercy-seat	159
Art thou weary, art thou languid	33
As now the sun's declining rays	125
As pants the heart for cooling streams	97
As when the weary traveller gains	159
As with gladness men of old	254

Index of Hymns.

	PAGE
At even, ere the sun was set	262
At the Cross, her station keeping	46
At the Lamb's high feast we sing	239
Awake, and sing the song	223
Awake, my soul, and with the sun	103
Be Thou my Guardian and my Guide	208
Before Jehovah's awful throne	114
Before the ending of the day	22
Begone unbelief, my Saviour is near	159
Behold the Lamb	243
Behold the Lamb of God, Who bore	229
Behold, the Master passeth by	105
Behold the mountain of the Lord	129
Behold us, Lord, before Thee met	258
Blessed city, heavenly Salem	89
Blest are the pure in heart	195
Blest Creator of the light	30
Blest day of God, how calm, how bright	84
Blow ye the trumpet, blow	148
Bound upon the accursèd tree	191
Bread of heaven, on Thee we feed	233
Bread of the world, in mercy broken	186
Brethren, let us join to bless	143
Brief life is here our portion	44
Bright the vision that delighted	181
Brightest and best of the sons of the morning	185
Brother, thou art gone before us	190
By cool Siloam's shady rill	187
By precepts taught of ages past	204
By the Cross, sad vigil keeping	46, 180
Captains of the saintly band	126
Children of the heavenly King	144
Christ is gone up; yet ere He passed	205
Christ is made the sure Foundation	89

	PAGE
Christ is our Corner Stone	89
Christ Jesus lay in Death's strong bands	70
Christ, the Lord, is risen again	249
Christ, the Lord, is risen to-day	145
Christ, Whose glory fills the skies	146
Christ will gather in His own	132
Christian, dost thou see them	221
Christian, seek not yet repose	201
Christians, awake, salute the happy morn	223
Come, gracious Spirit, heavenly Dove	223
Come, Holy Ghost, Creator blest	40
Come, Holy Ghost, eternal God	39
Come, Holy Ghost, our souls inspire	38
Come, Holy Ghost, Who ever One	213
Come, Holy Spirit, heavenly Dove	116, 223
Come, immortal King of Glory	145
Come, labour on	246
Come, let us join our cheerful songs	116
Come, let us join our friends above	147
Come, let us to the Lord our God	129
Come, Lord, and tarry not	210
Come, my soul, thy suit prepare	159
Come, O Thou Traveller unknown	149
Come, pure hearts, in sweetest measures	239
Come, see the place where Jesus lay	167
Come, take by faith the Body of the Lord	205
Come, Thou Holy Spirit, come	37
Come, Thou Holy Paraclete	37
Come, Thou long expected Jesus	148
Come to the morning prayer	172
Come unto Me, ye weary	255
Come, ye faithful, raise the anthem	231
Come, ye faithful, raise the strain	33
Come, ye saints, and raise an anthem	231
Come, ye thankful people, come	244
Commit thou all thy griefs	84

Index of Hymns.

	PAGE
Conquering kings their titles take	125
Creator of the world, to Thee	126
Creator of the starry height	205
Creator Spirit, by Whose aid	40
Crown Him with many crowns	242
Day of judgment, day of wonders	48, 159
Day of wrath, O day of mourning	47
Days and moments quickly flying	250
Dear Christian people, now rejoice	68
Deathless principle, arise	154
Disposer Supreme	125, 208
Draw nigh and take the Body of the Lord	205
Draw nigh, draw nigh, Emmanuel	205
Earth has many a noble city	26
Eternal Beam of Light Divine	152
Eternal Father, strong to save	254
Eternal Source of every joy	123
Exalted high, at God's right hand	229
Fair waved the golden corn	235
Far from my heavenly home	198
Far from the world, O Lord, I flee	158
Far from these narrow scenes of night	225
Father, again in Jesus' Name we meet	232
Father, by Thy love and power	235
Father, let me dedicate	248
Father of all, from land and sea	256
Father of all, in every age	119
Father of heaven, Whose love profound	231
Father of mercies, God of love	230
Father of mercies, in Thy Word	225
Father, whate'er of earthly bliss	225
Fear not, O little flock, the foe	80
Fierce raged the tempest o'er the deep	262

Index of Hymns.

	PAGE
Fierce was the wild billow	27
For all the Saints who from their labours rest	247
For all Thy Saints, O Lord	181
For ever with the Lord	171
For thee, O dear, dear country	44
For Thy dear Saint, O Lord	181
For Thy mercy and Thy grace	238
Forgive them, O my Father	209
Forth, in Thy Name, O Lord, I go	146
Forward, be our watchword	244
Fountain of good, to own Thy love	123
Fountain of mercy, God of love	230
From all that dwell below the skies	116
From all Thy saints in warfare	257
From Egypt lately come	167
From Greenland's icy mountains	183
From heaven above to earth I come	70
From highest heaven, the eternal Son	252
Gentle Jesu, meek and mild	148
Gentle Shepherd, Thou hast stilled	249
Give heed, my heart, lift up thine eyes	70
Give me the wings of faith to rise	116
Glorious things of thee are spoken	159
Glory be to Jesus	251
Glory to Thee, my God, this night	104
Glory to Thee, O Lord	242
Go forward, Christian soldier	248
Go, labour on; spend and be spent	210
Go to dark Gethsemane	171
God from on high hath heard	58
God moves in a mysterious way	157
God of mercy, God of grace	199
God of my life, to Thee I call	156
God of that glorious gift of grace	241
God, that madest earth and heaven	186

	PAGE
God the Father, Whose creation	205
Gracious Spirit, Holy Ghost	256
Great God, what do I see and hear	77
Great King of nations, hear our prayer	235
Great Mover of all hearts, Whose hand	208
Great Shepherd of Thy people, hear	159
Guide me, O Thou great Jehovah	227
Hail, gladdening Light	11, 197
Hail that Head, all torn and wounded	42
Hail the day that sees Him rise	148
Hail, Thou once despised Jesus	225
Hail, Thou Source of every blessing	231
Hail to the Lord's Anointed	170
Hark, a thrilling voice is sounding	22
Hark! hark, my soul, angelic songs are swelling	202
Hark, my soul! it is the Lord	156
Hark the glad sound! the Saviour comes	122
Hark! the herald angels sing	141
Hark! the song of Jubilee	172
Hark! the sound of holy voices	256
Have mercy, Lord, on me	96
Have mercy on us, God most High	203
He's gone. See where His body lay	167
He Who once in righteous vengeance	251
Head of the Church triumphant	148
Heal us, Emmanuel; hear our prayer	159
Here, O my Lord, I see Thee face to face	210
High let us swell our tuneful notes	122
His are the thousand sparkling rills	209
Holy, Holy, Holy, Lord God Almighty	185
Holy offerings, rich and rare	241
Hosanna to the living Lord	185
How are Thy servants blest, O Lord	98
How beauteous are their feet	116
How blessed from the bonds of sin	245

	PAGE
How blessed Thy creature is, O God	158
How bright appears the Morning Star	79
How bright these glorious spirits shine	129
How sweet the Name of Jesus sounds	159
How vain the cruel Herod's fear	205
Hues of the rich unfolding morn	194
I could not do without Thee	215
I gave My life for thee	216
I heard the voice of Jesus say	210
I lay my sins on Jesus	210
I need Thee, precious Jesu	252
I praised the earth in beauty seen	187
I was a wandering sheep	210
I'll praise my Maker while I've breath	115
I thirst, Thou wounded Lamb of God	137
In evil long I took delight	158
In grief and fear, to Thee, O Lord	245
In the hour of trial	172
In the Lord's atoning grief	46
In the midst of life we are in death	36
In Thy Name, O Lord, assembling	167
In token that thou shalt not fear	243
Is thy cruse of comfort wasting	13
It came upon the midnight clear	242
It is finished; Blessed Jesus	260
It was the winter wild	90
Jerusalem, my happy home	86
Jerusalem on high	222
Jerusalem the golden	45
Jesu, Lover of my soul	142
Jesu, meek and gentle	251
Jesu, meek and lowly	243
Jesu, my Lord, my God, my All	243
Jesu, my strength, my hope	148

	PAGE
Jesu, our Hope, our heart's Desire	237
Jesu, still lead on	132
Jesu, Sun of Righteousness	246
Jesu, the very thought is sweet	40
Jesu, the very thought of Thee	40
Jesu, these eyes have never seen	41
Jesu, Thou joy of loving hearts	40
Jesu, Thou wounded Lamb of God	137
Jesu, Thy blood and righteousness	132
Jesu, Thy mercies are untold	41
Jesu, where'er Thy people meet	158
Jesus calls us; o'er the tumult	209
Jesus Christ is risen to-day	146
Jesus, I my cross have taken	199
Jesus, I will trust Thee	217
Jesus is God; the solid earth	203
Jesus lives! no longer now	224
Jesus, my Lord, how rich Thy grace	123
Jesus, my Redeemer, lives	83
Jesus, Name of wondrous love	247
Jesus shall reign where'er the sun	116
Join all the glorious names	116
Joy! because the circling year	261
Joy fills our inmost heart to-day	255
Joy to the world! The Lord is come	116
Just as I am, without one plea	201
King of saints, Almighty Word	9
Lead, kindly Light	212
Lead us, heavenly Father lead us	232
Let all the world in every corner sing	85
Let me be with Thee where Thou art	201
Let our choir new anthems raise	34
Let saints on earth in concert sing	147
Let this our solemn Feast	59
Let us with a gladsome mind	90

Index of Hymns.

	PAGE
Lift the strain of high thanksgiving	261
Lift up your heads, ye gates of brass	173
Light's abode, celestial Salem	205
Light's glittering morn bedecks the sky	22
Lo! God is here; let us adore	136
Lo! He comes with clouds descending	143
Lo! He cometh, countless trumpets	144
Lo! now is our accepted day	29
Lo! round the Throne, a glorious band	229
Lo! the angels' Food is given	59
Lo! the storms of life are breaking	244
Long did I toil, and knew no earthly rest	199
Lord, as to Thy dear Cross we flee	235
Lord, cause Thy face on us to shine	123
Lord, dismiss us with Thy blessing	229
Lord God, the Holy Ghost	173
Lord, her watch Thy Church is keeping	238
Lord, in this Thy mercy's day	208
Lord, in Thy Name Thy servants plead	196
Lord, it belongs not to my care	92
Lord Jesus, think on me	16
Lord of mercy and of might	187
Lord of our life and God of our salvation	245
Lord of the harvest, once again	235
Lord of the harvest, Thee we hail	235
Lord of the Sabbath, hear our vows	123
Lord of the Sabbath, hear us pray	123
Lord of the worlds above	116
Lord, pour Thy Spirit from on high	171
Lord, speak to me, that I may speak	215
Lord, teach us how to pray aright	173
Lord, Thy Word abideth	253
Lord, to whom except to Thee	240
Lord, when Thy Kingdom comes, remember me	260
Lord, when we bend before Thy throne	177
Love Divine, all love excelling	148

Index of Hymns.

	PAGE
Maker of all things, God most High	19
May the grace of Christ our Saviour	159
Mighty Father, Blessed Son	241
Morn of morns and day of days	208
Morn of morns, the best and first	209
Much in sorrow, oft in woe	179
My faith looks up to Thee	41
My God, accept my heart this day	243
My God and Father, while I stray	201
My God, and is Thy Table spread	122
My God, how wonderful Thou art	204
My God, I love Thee, not because	221
My God, is any hour so sweet	201
My God, now I from sleep awake	102
My God, the spring of all my joys	116
My Lord, my Love was crucified	203
My Saviour, can it ever be	197
My soul doth magnify the Lord	197
Nearer, my God, to Thee	236
New every morning is the love	194
No; not despairingly	210
No sign we ask from heaven above	248
Not all the blood of beasts	117
Not unto us, but Thee, O Lord	144
Now, gracious Lord, Thine arm reveal	159
Now I have found the ground wherein	137
Now it belongs not to my care	92
Now, my soul, thy voice upraising	125
Now, my tongue, the mystery telling	58
Now thank we all our God	82
Now that the daylight dies away	213
Now that the daylight fills the sky	20
Now the day is over	211
Now the labourer's task is o'er	261

Index of Hymns.

	PAGE
O bless the Lord, my soul	117
O Brightness of the Eternal Father's face	11
O brothers, lift your voices	259
O Christ, Redeemer of our race	22
O Christ, Who art the Light and Day	22
O Christ, Who hast prepared a place	126
O come, all ye faithful	236
O come and mourn with me a while	203
O come, loud anthems let us sing	97
O come, O come, Emmanuel	205
O come, Redeemer of mankind, appear	21
O day, most calm, most bright	84
O day of rest and gladness	256
O Father, Thou Who hast created all	249
O for a closer walk with God	157
O for a faith that will not shrink	233
O for a heart to praise my God	148
O for a thousand tongues to sing	148
O God of Bethel, by Whose hand	123
O God of Hosts, the mighty Lord	96
O God of Jacob, by Whose hand	123
O God, our help in ages past	114
O God, the Rock of Ages	259
O God, Thou art my God alone	173
O God, Thy soldiers' great reward	22
O God, unseen, yet ever near	234
O happy band of pilgrims	34
O happy day that fixed my choice	123
O heavenly Jerusalem	208
O heavenly Word, eternal Light	59
O help us, Lord; each hour of need	190
O Holy Ghost, Thou God of peace	208
O Holy Saviour, Friend unseen	201
O Holy Spirit, Lord of grace	126
O Jesu, ever present	248
O Jesu, I have promised	258

P.

	PAGE
O Jesu, King most wonderful	41
O Jesu, Lord of heavenly grace	20
O Jesu, Thou art standing	246
O Jesu, Thou the Beauty art	41
O let him whose sorrow	230
O Lord, another day is flown	179
O Lord, how happy should we be	234
O Lord, how joyful 'tis to see	126
O Lord most High, Eternal King	20
O Lord, my God, do Thou Thy holy will	197
O Lord of heaven and earth and sea	256
O Lord, our languid souls inspire	159
O Lord, turn not Thy face away	222
O Lord, within Thy sacred gates	137
O Love divine, how sweet Thou art	143
O Love, how deep, how broad, how high	206
O Love, Who formedst me to wear	248
O merciful Creator, hear	29
O Morning Star, how fair and bright	79
O mother dear, Jerusalem	86
O Paradise, O Paradise	202
O praise our great and gracious Lord	207
O quickly come, dread Judge of all	247
O render thanks to God above	97
O sacred Head, once wounded	41
O sacred Head, surrounded	41
O Saviour, is Thy promise fled	186
O Saviour Lord, to Thee we pray	60
O Saviour, may we never rest	233
O Saviour, precious Saviour	216
O Saviour, Who for man hast trod	126
O sons and daughters, let us sing	206
O Spirit of the living God	172
O Strength and Stay, upholding all creation	261
O Thou, from Whom all goodness flows	228
O Thou, the contrite sinner's Friend	202

	PAGE
O Thou, to Whose all-searching sight	137
O Thou, Who camest from above	148
O Trinity, most blessed Light	20
O what, if we are Christ's	253
O what the joy and the glory must be	206
O where shall rest be found	173
O Word of God Incarnate	247
O worship the King	188
O'er the gloomy hills of darkness	227
O'erwhelmed in depths of woe	251
Of the Father's love begotten	25
Oft in danger, oft in woe	179
On Jordan's banks, the Baptist's cry	125
On the mountain's top appearing	167
On the Resurrection morning	211
On the waters dark and drear	255
On this day, the first of days	29
On this day when days began	29
Once in David's royal city	209
Once more the solemn season calls	126
Once, only once, and once for all	258
Onward, Christian soldiers	211
Our blest Redeemer, ere He breathed	207
Our day of praise is done	261
Our God, our help in ages past	114
Our Lord is risen from the dead	149
Out of the deep I call	253
Out of the depths I cry to Thee	69
Palms of glory, raiment bright	173
Peace, perfect peace, in this dark world of sin	259
Pleasant are Thy courts above	198
Pour out Thy Spirit from on high	171
Praise, my soul, the King of heaven	199
Praise, O praise our God and King	90
Praise the Lord, His glories show	199

18—2

	PAGE
Praise the Lord through every nation	173
Praise to God, immortal praise	226
Praise to the Holiest in the height	213
Praise the Lord! ye heavens, adore Him	232
Prayer is the soul's sincere desire	173
Redeemer of the nations, come	21
Rejoice, all ye believers	246
Rejoice to-day with one accord	67, 253
Rejoice, the Lord is King	143, 149
Rejoice, ye pure in heart	257
Rest of the weary, joy of the sad	241
Ride on! ride on in majesty	189
Rock of Ages, cleft for me	152
Round the Lord, in glory seated	181
Safe home, safe home in port	34
Salvation, O the joyful sound	117
Saviour, again to Thy dear Name we raise	260
Saviour, Blessed Saviour	262
Saviour, breathe an evening blessing	232
Saviour, sprinkle many nations	241
Saviour, when in dust to Thee	188
See the Conqueror mounts in triumph	256
See the destined day arise	180
Servant of God, well done	173
Shepherd Divine, our wants relieve	149
Sinful, sighing to be blest	241
Sing Alleluia forth in duteous praise	61
Sing, my tongue, the glorious battle	28
Sing, my tongue, the Saviour's glory	28
Sing to the Lord a joyful song	241
Sing to the Lord with cheerful voice	115
Sing we triumphant songs of praise	31
Sinners, turn, why will ye die	149
Sleepers, wake, a voice is calling	78

Index of Hymns.

	PAGE
Soldiers of Christ, arise	149
Sometimes a light surprises	156
Son of Man, to Thee I cry	181
Songs of praise the Angels sang	172
Songs of thankfulness and praise	256
Sons of men, behold from far	149
Souls of men, why will ye scatter	204
Sow in the morn thy seed	173
Speed Thy servants, Saviour, speed them	167
Spirit of mercy, truth and love	228
Spirit of truth, on this Thy day	187
Stand up and bless the Lord	173
Stars of the morning, so gloriously bright	34
Sun of my soul, Thou Saviour dear	195
Sweet day, so cool, so calm, so bright	84
Sweet flowerets of the martyr band	26
Sweet is the work, my God, my King	117
Sweet place, sweet place alone	222
Sweet Saviour, bless us ere we go	203
Sweet the moments, rich in blessing	226
Take up thy cross, the Saviour said	233
Ten thousand times ten thousand	244
Tender Shepherd, Thou hast stilled	249
That day of wrath, that dreadful day	48
The Advent of our King	125
The Church has waited long	210
The Church's one foundation	50
The day is past and over	26
The day, O Lord, is spent	206
The day of Resurrection	33
The eternal gifts of Christ the King	22
The God of Abraham praise	150
The God, Whom earth and sea and sky	28
The great forerunner of the morn	30
The happy morn is come	229

	PAGE
The Head that once was crowned with thorns	167
The heavenly Child in stature grows	126
The heavenly Word proceeding forth	59
The heavens declare Thy glory, Lord	117
<u>The King of love my Shepherd is</u>	253
The Lamb's high banquet called to share	22
The Lord is King, lift up thy voice	234
The Lord my pasture shall prepare	100
The Lord of Might from Sinai's brow	187
The Lord will come; the earth shall quake	187
The people that in darkness sat	129
The race that long in darkness pined	129
The radiant morn hath passed away	262
The roseate hues of early dawn	209
The Royal banners forward go	27
The Royal banner is unfurled	28
The Saints of God, their conflict past	259
The saints on earth and those above	147
The Son of God goes forth to war	185
The spacious firmament on high	100
The strain upraise of joy and praise	35
The strife is o'er, the battle done	260
The sun is sinking fast	251
The voice that breathed o'er Eden	197
The world is very evil	45
The year begins with Thee	197
The year is gone beyond recall	260
Thee we adore, O hidden Saviour, Thee	58
Thee will I love, my strength, my tower	137
There is a blessèd home	252
There is a book, who runs may read	195
There is a fountain filled with blood	156
There is a green hill far away	209
There is a land of pure delight	111
There is a Name I love to hear	252
There is a stream which issues forth	197

Index of Hymns.

	PAGE
These glorious minds how bright they shine	129
They come, God's messengers of love	238
Thine arm, O Lord, in days of old	257
Thine for ever! God of love	238
This is the day of light	261
This is the day the Lord hath made	117
Those eternal bowers	32
Thou art coming, O my Saviour	215
Thou art gone to the grave	187
Thou art gone up on high	242
Thou'rt mine, yes, still thou art mine own	84
Thou art the Way; to Thee alone	233
Thou bounteous Giver of the light	24
Thou glorious Sun of righteousness	202
Thou hidden love of God, Whose height	137
Thou Judge of quick and dead	146
Thou, Lord, by strictest search hast known	97
Thou, to Whom the sick and dying	262
Thou, Whose Almighty word	207
Three in One, and One in Three	240
Through all the changing scenes of life	96
Through midnight gloom from Macedon	50
Through the day Thy love has spared us	167
Through the night of doubt and sorrow	211
Thy Life was given for me	216
Thy way, not mine, O Lord	210
'Tis done, that new and heavenly birth	253
'Tis gone, that bright and orbèd blaze	195
To bless Thy chosen race	96
To morrow, Lord, is Thine	123
To the Name that brings salvation	206
To Thee, O Comforter Divine	216
To Thee, O Lord, our hearts we raise	255
To Thee, our God, we fly	247
To Thy temple I repair	173
Toss'd with rough winds, and faint with fear	13

	PAGE
Vital spark of heavenly flame	118
Wake, awake, for night is flying	79
We are but little children weak	209
We give immortal praise	117
We give Thee but Thine own	247
We love the place, O God	244
We plough the fields and scatter	255
We saw Thee not when Thou didst come	236
We sing the praise of Him Who died	166
Weary of earth and laden with my sin	50
Welcome, happy morning	261
We've no abiding city here	167
What are these in bright array	173
What happy men or angels these	129
What our Father does is well	253
What star is this with beams so bright	126
What though my frail eyelids refuse	154
What various hindrances we meet	158
When all Thy mercies, O my God	100
When at Thy footstool, Lord, I bend	199
When gathering clouds around I view	188
When God of old came down from heaven	195
When I can read my title clear	111
When I survey life's varied scene	226
When I survey the wondrous Cross	114
When languor and disease invade	153
When morning gilds the skies	251
When our heads are bowed with woe	190
When rising from the bed of death	100
When the Architect Almighty	257
When through the torn sail	187
When wounded sore the stricken soul	209
Where high the heavenly temple stands	128
While my Jesus I'm possessing	226
While shepherds watched their flocks by night	96

Index of Hymns.

	PAGE
Who are these like stars appearing	224
Who is this so weak and helpless	247
Why should I fear the darkest hour	159
Why those fears? Behold 'tis Jesus	167
With glory clad, with strength arrayed	97
With joy we meditate the grace	117
With one consent let all the earth	97
Word Supreme, before creation	197
Ye boundless realms of joy	96
Ye choirs of New Jerusalem	239
Ye faithful, approach ye	237
Ye holy angels bright	93
Ye servants of God	149
Ye servants of our glorious King	240
Ye servants of the Lord	122
Yes, God is good; in earth and sky	236
Yesterday, with exultation	45
Your harps, ye trembling saints	153

LATIN HYMNS AND SEQUENCES.

The addition of the Letters S *or* Y *denotes that the Hymn or Sequence occurs respectively in the Sarum and York Service Books, chiefly in the Breviary or Missal.*

Ad cœnam Agni providi	S. Y.	22, 239
Ad regias Agni dapes		239
Adeste fideles		236
Adoro Te devote, latens Deitas		58
Æterna Christi munera	Y.	22, 240
Æterne rerum Conditor	S.	21
Æterne Rex, Altissime	S. Y.	20

Index of Hymns.

	PAGE
Alleluia, dulce carmen (Anglo-Saxon Hymnaries)	60
Alleluia perenne (,, ,,)	61
Alleluia piis edite laudibus (,, ,,)	61
Angulare fundamentum lapis Christus missus est Y.	89
Apparuit benignitas	206
Aurora lucis rutilat S. Y.	22
Audi, benigne Conditor S. Y.	29
Beata nobis gaudia S. Y.	261
Cantemus cuncti melodum nunc, Alleluia	35
Chorus Novæ Jerusalem S. Y.	239
Christe, qui Lux es et Dies S. Y.	22
Christe, Redemptor omnium S. Y.	22
Christo profusum sanguinem	240
Cœlestis O Jerusalem	208
Cœlestis urbs, Jerusalem	88
Conditor almæ siderum S. Y.	205
Corde natus, ex Parentis Y.	25
Creator alme siderum	205
Deus, Creator omnium S. Y.	20
Deus, Tuorum militum Y.	22
Die dierum principe	208
Die parente temporum	29
Dies iræ, dies illa S.	47, 78
Ecce panis angelorum S. Y.	59
Ecce tempus idoneum S.	29
En clara vox redarguit	22
Ex more docti mystico S. Y.	205
Finita jam sunt prælia	260
Gloria, laus et honor Tibi S. Y.	34
Gloriosi Salvatoris nominis	206
Hic breve vivitur	44

Index of Hymns. 283

	PAGE
Heri mundus exultavit	45
Hora novissima	44
Hostis Herodes impie S. Y.	205
Hymnum canamus gloriæ Y.	31
Hymnum canentes martyrum	31
In Passione Domini	46
Ira justa Conditoris	251
Jam Christus astra ascenderat S. Y.	250
Jam desinant suspiria	58
Jam lucis orto sidere S. Y.	20
Jam surgit hora tertia	21
Jerusalem luminosa	206
Jesu, dulcis memoria	41
Jesu, nostra redemptio S. Y.	237
Jesus refulsit omnium	57
Jucundare plebs fidelis Y.	239
Lauda Sion Salvatorem S. Y.	59
Lucis Creator optime S. Y.	30
Lucis Largitor splendide	24
Lustra sex qui jam peregit (peracta S. Y.)	181
Media vita in morte sumus S. Y.	36
Nunc Sancte, nobis, Spiritus S. Y.	213
O bona patria	44
O Deus, ego amo Te	221
O filii et filiæ	206
O Lux beata, Trinitas S. Y.	20, 240
O sola magnarum urbium	26
Pange lingua gloriosi lauream certaminis	181
Pange lingua gloriosi prœlium certaminis S. Y.	28, 181
Pange lingua gloriosi Corporis mysterium S. Y.	58
Precursor altus luminis	30

Index of Hymns.

	PAGE
Primo dierum omnium S. Y.	29
Psallat chorus corde mundo Y.	239
Quem terra, pontus, æthera S. Y.	28
Quicunque certum quæritis.	251
Rerum Deus tenax vigor S. Y.	261
Sacris solemniis juncta sint gaudia S. Y.	59
Sævo dolorem turbine.	251
Salvator mundi, Domine S. Y.	60
Salve Caput cruentatum	41
Salve festa dies S. Y.	28, 262
Salve, mundi salutare.	42
Salvete flores martyrum	26
Sancti venite, Christi Corpus sumite.	205
Splendor Paternæ gloriæ S. Y.	20
Stabat Mater dolorosa.	46, 180
Supreme Motor cordium	208
Surrexit Christus hodie	146
Te Deum laudamus S. Y.	23
Te lucis ante terminum S. Y.	22, 213
Tu, Trinitatis Unitas S. Y.	240
Urbs beata, Jerusalem Y.	88
Urbs Syon aurea.	45
Veni, Creator Spiritus S. Y.	38
Veni, Redemptor gentium S. Y.	21
Veni, Sancte Spiritus S. Y.	37
Veni, veni, Emmanuel.	205
Verbum supernum prodiens, A Patre S. Y.	59
Verbum supernum prodiens, Nec Patris S. Y.	59
Vexilla Regis prodeunt S. Y.	27
Vox clara ecce intonat S. Y.	22

Index of Hymns.

GERMAN HYMNS.

	PAGE
Aller Gläubigen Sammelplatz	132
Aus tiefer Noth schrei ich zu Dir	69
Befiehl du deine Wege	84
Christ lag in Todesbanden	70
Christi Blut und Gerechtigkeit	132
Christe, Du Beistand Deiner Kreuzgemeine	245
Christus ist erstanden	249
Du bist zwar mein und bleibest mein	84
Ein feste Burg ist unser Gott	64
Ermuntert euch, ihr Frommen	246
Es ist gewisslich an der Zeit	78
Gott ist gegenwärtig! lasset uns anbeten	137
Guter Hirt, Du hast gestillt	250
Ich habe nun den Grund gefunden	137
Ich will Dich lieben, meine Stärke	137
In Christi Wunden schlaf ich ein	132
Jesu, geh voran	133
Jesus lebt, mit Ihm auch ich	224
Jesus, meine Zuversicht	83
Komm, Heidenheiland, Löseheld	21
Liebe, die du mich zum Bilde	248
Mitten wir im Leben sind	37
Morgenglanz der Ewigkeit	246

	PAGE
Nun danket alle Gott	81
Nun freut euch, lieben Christen gemein	68
O Haupt, voll Blut und Wunden	42
O Vaterherz, das Erd und Himmel schuf	249
Seelenbräutigam, O Du Gottes Lamm	137
Verborgne Gottes Liebe, Du	137
Verzage nicht, O Häuflein klein	80
Vom Himmel hoch da komm Ich her	70
Wachet auf! ruft uns die Stimme	78
Was Gott thut, das ist wohlgethan	254
Wenn in Leidenstagen	230
Wer sind die vor Gottes Throne	224
Wie schön leuchtet der Morgenstern	79
Wir pflügen und wir streuen	255

GENERAL INDEX.

The principal references only are given.

Adam of S. Victor, 45, 239
Adams, Sarah, 236
Addison, Joseph, 97
Alexander, Frances, 209
Alexander, J. W., 41
Alexander, W. L., 10
Alford, Dean, 42, 243
Alleluia, 36, 61
Allen, James, 226
Alteration of hymns, 174, 190
Ambrose, 17
Ambrosian hymns, 22
Anatolius, 26, 57
Andrew of Crete, 221
Angelus Silesius, 137, 248
Anstice, Joseph, 197, 234
Aquinas, Thomas, 58
Aratus, 56
Auber, Harriet, 207
Augustine, 18, 21, 56

Baker, Francis, 87
Baker, Sir H. W., 90, 252
Bakewell, John, 225
Barbauld, Letitia, 226
Bardesanes, 11

Baring-Gould, S., 211
Bathurst, W. H., 233
Baxter, Richard, 91
Bede, Venerable, 30
Benson, Archp., 89
Bernard of Clairvaux, 40
Bernard of Clugny, 43
Bickersteth, Bishop, 259
Bode, J. E., 258
Bohemian Brethren, 130
Bonar, Horatius, 210
Bonaventura, 45
Borthwick, Jane, 133, 245
Brady, Nicholas, 95
Breviary, Mozarabic, 61; Paris, 124; Roman, 61; Sarum, 20, 23, 39, 60, 186; York, 186
Bridges, Matthew, 243
Bright, William, 258
Browne, Simon, 223
Bruce, Michael, 129
Bullock, Dean, 244
Bunsen's *Gesangbuch*, 79
Byrom, John, 223

Cameron, William, 129

Campbell, J. M., 255
Carlyle, J. D., 177
Caswall, Edward, 250
Cennick, John, 143
Chambers, J. D., 59
Chandler, John, 237
Charlemagne, 38
Charles, Elizabeth, 13
Chatfield, A. W., 16
Christian Year, 192
Chrysostom, 14
Claudius, Matthias, 255
Clement, 9
Codex Alexandrinus, 8, 23
Coffin, Charles, 58, 124, 208
Collins, Henry, 243
Collyer, W. B., 77, 179
Conder, Josiah, 234
Cooper, Edward, 231
Copeland, W. J., 22, 60
Cosin, Bishop, 39
Cotterill, Thos., 123, 175, 230
Cox, Frances, 224
Coxe, Bishop, 241
Cowper, William, 154
Crossman, Samuel, 222

Dayman, E. A., 79
Dickson, David, 86
Dies Iræ, 47, 78
Dix, W. C., 254
Doane, Bishop, 233
Doddridge, Philip, 120
Downton, Henry, 238
Dryden, John, 40

Eber, Paul, 132

Eddis, E. W., 11
Edmeston, James, 232
Ellerton, John, 29, 61, 260
Elliott, Charlotte, 200
Ephrem the Syrian, 12
Everest, C. W., 233

Faber, F. W., 202
Fawcett, John, 229
Feith, Rhijnvis, 173
Flowerdew, Alice, 230
Franck, Johann, 21
Fulbert of Chartres, 239

Gaskell, W., 66
Gellert, C. F., 224
Gerhardt, Paul, 42, 83
Giovani di Fidenza, 46
Godescalcus, 35
Grant, Sir R., 188
Gregory the Great, 28, 38
Gurney, J. H., 235
Gustavus Adolphus, 80

Hammond, William, 223
Harmonius, 12
Havergal, F. R., 214
Haweis, Thomas, 228
Heber, Bishop, 181, 222
Herbert, George, 84
Hilary, 24, 57
Hill, Rowland, 229
Hopkins, John, 73
How, Bishop Walsham, 246
Hupton, Job, 231
Hymn, definition of, 56
Hymnary, Roman, 62, 124

Hymns, alteration of, 174, 190;
  Ambrosian, 22; Arian, 14;
  distinguished from psalms,
  56; earliest Christian, 7;
  Gnostic, 11; Moravian, 133;
  Olney, 156; sanctioned, 72;
  Wesleyan, 136

Ingemann, B. S., 211
Irons, W. J., 47

Jacobus de Benedictis, 47
Jacopone da Todi, 47
James I., 94
Jewish Hymnody, 5
John Damascene, 31
Joseph of the Studium, 33

Keble, John, 11, 191
Kelly, Thomas, 166
Kempthorne, John, 232
Ken, Bishop, 102
Kethe, William, 76
Knapp, Albert, 249
Koch, *Geschichte*, 78

Langton, Archp., 37
Laurenti, L., 246
Leeson, J. E., 145
Logan, John, 123, 130
Louisa, Electress, 83
Löwenstern, v. M. A., 245
Luther, Martin, 37, 43, 63, 82
Lyte, H. F., 198

Maclagan, Bishop, 259
Madan, Martin, 142, 143

P.

Maitland, F. Fuller-, 179
Mant, Bishop, 46, 180
Marckant, John, 222
Marot, Clément, 71
Marriott, John, 207
Marvell, Andrew, 101
Mason, John, 84, 197, 203
Massie, Richard, 70
Maude, M. F., 238
Meinhold, J. W., 250
Mercer, William, 79
Milman, Dean, 189
Milton, John, 89
Missal, Sarum, 35, 48
Monsell, S. B., 240
Montgomery, James, 168, 175
Moravians, 130, 140, 168
Morgan, D. T., 21
Morrison, John, 129

Neale, J. M., 44, 204
Nelson, Earl, 257
Newman, Cardinal, 211
Newton, John, 48, 155, 158
Nicolai, Philipp, 78
Notker, 36

Oakeley, Frederick, 46, 237
Olivers, Thos., 145, 149, 225
Osler, Edward, 123, 234
Oswald, H. S., 230

Palmer, Ray, 41
Paraphrases, 128
Paris Breviary, 124
Perronet, Edward, 228
Plumptre, Dean, 257

19

Pope, Alexander, 118
Pott, Francis, 260
Prayer Book, 39, 62, 93
Prose, 36, 48
Prudentius, 25
Prynne, G. R., 251
Psalm, definition of, 56
Psalms, Marot's, 71; New Version of, 94, 122; Old Version of, 73, 89, 127, 222
Psalter, Daye's, 74; French, 76; Scotch, 76, 127
Pusey, Philip, 245

Rhyme, 57
Ringwaldt, Barthol., 77
Rinkart, Martin, 82
Robert II. of France, 37
Roman Breviary, 61
Rorison, Gilbert, 240
Rosenroth, v. K., 246
Rothe, J. A., 137
Rouse, Francis, 94, 127

Santeuil, de, Claude, 125
Santeuil, de, J. B., 124
Santolius Maglorianus, 125
Santolius Victorinus, 124
Sarum Breviary, 20, 23, 39, 60, 186
Sarum Missal, 35, 48
Scheffler, Johann, 248
Schenk, H. T., 224
Schmolck, Benjamin, 254
Scotch Psalter, 76, 127
Scott, Sir W., 47, 126, 182

Sears, E. H., 242
Sequence, 36; Alleluiatic, 35; Golden, 37
Shirley, Walter, 226
Songs, spiritual, 6, 56
Spectator, The, 98, 119
Stabat Mater, 46, 180
Steele, Anne, 225
Stephen the Sabaite, 33
Sternhold, Thomas, 72
Stone, S. J., 50
Synesius, 15

Tate, Nahum, 95
Te Deum, 23
Ter Sanctus, 8, 23
Tersteegen, Gerhard, 137
Theodulph, 34
Thomas of Celano, 47
Thring, Godfrey, 262
Toke, Emma, 242
Toplady, A. M., 151
Trisagion, 8
Tuttiett, Lawrence, 247
Twells, Henry, 262

Venantius Fortunatus, 27, 181, 261
Veni Creator, 38
Version, New, 94, 122; Old, 73, 127, 222

Walker, M. J., 217
Watts, Isaac, 110, 129, 147
Weiss, Michael, 249
Wesley, Charles, 112, 134, 141
Wesley, John, 115, 134, 151

Wesleys' Collection, 115, 136
Whateley, Archp., 186, 193
White, H. K., 178
Whitfield, Frederick, 252
Whiting, William, 254
Whitmore, Lady Lucy, 232
Williams, Isaac, 208
Williams, William, 227

Winkworth, Catherine, 21, 132, 248
Woodford, Bishop, 58
Woodd, Basil, 231
Wordsworth, Bishop, 256

Xavier, Francis, 221

Zinzendorf, von, 130, 135, 216

www.ingramcontent.com/pod-product-compliance
Lightning Source LLC
Chambersburg PA
CBHW022101230426
43672CB00008B/1248